STACKED

The No-BS System to Stack Skills,
Build Leverage, and Become Unstoppable

SEARS KEPLAR, MBA

Living Book Technology™ is a trademark of Stacked Media Group LLC.

First Edition

ISBNs:
Paperback: 979-8-9934335-0-9
Hardcover: 979-8-9934335-9-2

Published by
YPAR Publishing
United States of America

YPAR Publishing is an imprint of Stacked Media Group LLC.

Printed in the United States of America

DISCLAIMER

This is not a finance or trading book. The ideas, frameworks, and stories presented are for educational and personal development purposes only. Nothing in this book should be interpreted as financial, investment, tax, legal, or accounting advice, nor as a recommendation to buy, sell, or trade any particular securities or financial instruments.

While the author holds a Series 65 license (as of the writing of this book) and has experience in financial education, the content herein reflects general concepts about skill development, reinvention, and decision-making—not personalized financial guidance.

Readers should consult licensed financial professionals before making any investment or financial decisions. Past performance is not indicative of future results, and all investing involves risk, including possible loss of principal. The author and publisher expressly disclaim any liability for actions taken or not taken based on this material.

The information provided in this book is for educational and informational purposes only and is not intended as medical advice, diagnosis, or treatment. The author is not a physician, and the content herein should not be construed as a substitute for professional medical judgment, diagnosis, or treatment.

Always seek the advice of a qualified physician or other licensed healthcare provider with any questions you may have regarding a medical condition, symptoms, or treatment options. Never disregard professional medical advice or delay seeking it because of something you have read in this book.

The author and publisher make no representations or warranties, express or implied, regarding the accuracy, completeness, applicability, or suitability of the information contained in this book for any individual or situation. Medical knowledge, standards of care, and best practices continually evolve; therefore, information presented may become outdated.

The author and publisher expressly disclaim any and all liability for any loss, injury, or damage—direct or indirect—arising from the use, misuse, or reliance upon any information contained in this book. Use of this material is solely at the reader's own risk.

This book does not establish a doctor–patient, therapist–patient, or other healthcare professional relationship between the reader and the author or publisher.

If you believe you may be experiencing a medical emergency, contact your physician, local emergency services, or emergency medical personnel immediately.

DEDICATION

To my "Nice Niece" McKayla, the smartest girl I know. I'm so proud of the woman you're becoming. I love you.

ABOUT THE AUTHOR

Sears Keplar turns complex financial concepts into actionable strategies for thousands of students nationwide. A Series 65 license holder and CMT Level 1 candidate, he specializes in options, futures, and crypto trading, known for blending rigorous risk management with teaching that sticks.

His path was anything but straight. Early jobs from Six Flags ride operator to Starbucks barista taught customer service and systems thinking, skills that later became the backbone of his ventures. After the 2008 real estate crash forced a pivot, Sears co-founded FlashPants, scaling it into California's most booked 80s band with multiple casts and national TV appearances. When COVID wiped out live entertainment, he reinvented again, this time in finance, proving that skills really do stack across industries.

As an entrepreneur, he has scaled multiple companies, from entertainment to marketing, by leveraging expertise in sales, branding, and systems design. Long before earning his MBA, Sears was already building frameworks and automation to grow teams and businesses. He has managed more than 25 entertainers across states, coached entrepreneurs, and mentored students on how to use skill stacking as a tool for reinvention.

Beyond business, Sears has explored personal development and healing practices including bodywork, energy work, and breathwork, adding depth to his understanding of resilience and performance. His story includes both extremes: living lean through seasons of credit defaults and car living, and living large with sailing to Catalina, racing the coast in his Porsche, grilling legendary steaks, mastering country two step, and even converting a van into a mobile home for someone without shelter. Every skill from welding in a makerspace to hosting dinner parties for CEOs reinforces his core philosophy: every skill stacks, and every stack builds leverage. He expands on this philosophy in his book, available at StackedBook.com.

Sears has dealt with more setbacks than most people face in a lifetime. He's lived out of his car, knocked on thousands of doors, and had entire businesses disappear overnight. He's also faced health scares and burnout that forced him to regroup and rise stronger. All those failures taught him things you can't learn in business school. Now when problems hit, he knows how to handle them because he's been through worse.

Today, he teaches, writes, and speaks with a single mission: showing others how to use reinvention as their greatest tool. He lives in Newport Beach, Corona del Mar, California, where he continues to add to his ever-growing stack. Connect with him at SearsKeplar.com or explore his book at StackedBook.com.

SEARS KEPLAR — KEYNOTE SPEAKER & FACILITATOR

Sears is a transformational speaker and educator known for blending strategy, psychology, and human performance into clear, actionable frameworks. His work spans entrepreneurship, leadership, real estate, entertainment, systems building, and market education. Sears doesn't deliver motivation—he shifts identity, decision-making, and performance.

Ideal for organizations, teams, and events navigating growth, change, or reinvention.

WHAT SEARS DELIVERS

- High-impact keynotes
- Interactive workshops & breakouts
- Executive off-sites & strategy days
- Conferences, retreats, and summits
- Virtual or in-person programs

All sessions are custom-built for the audience.

SIGNATURE TOPICS INCLUDE

- Skill Stacking & Personal Leverage
- Leadership Psychology & Presence
- Reinvention & Identity Shifts
- Behavioral Psychology for Investors & High-Performance Roles

AUDIENCES

- Corporate & executive teams
- Entrepreneurs & founders
- Investment groups, hedge funds & finance conferences
- Men's retreats & personal development events

WHY ORGANIZATIONS BOOK SEARS

- Strategy + human depth
- No fluff, high clarity
- Universal frameworks across industries
- Engaging presence with practical takeaways
- Talks that create lasting behavioral change

BOOKING

Email: booking@SearsKeplar.com or visit SearsKeplar.com

ABOUT LIVING BOOK TECHNOLOGY™

This book is part of the first generation of titles designed for Living Book Technology™ (Patent Pending), a new AI platform created to change the way readers learn, engage with, and apply the ideas inside a book.

Living Book Technology™ is not inside the physical pages you are holding. It is the system being built alongside this book, and this title serves as the first full integration and foundational test case for the platform.

The concept is simple. Authors and publishers upload their manuscripts into a dedicated AI environment that understands a book at a deep, structural level. Once inside the system, readers will be able to interact with the material as if it were a guide. You will be able to ask questions, clarify concepts, and explore how different chapters relate to your current challenges or goals. The AI responds using the actual frameworks, philosophy, and methodology found in these pages. It is not generic artificial intelligence. It is built from this manuscript and shaped by the spirit and architecture of the ideas behind it.

As the platform rolls out, Living Book Technology™ is designed to help readers break down complex concepts and walk through steps with precision. If you want help understanding your current transition stage, identifying your skill stack, designing your next move, or working through the book's exercises, the AI is intended to act as a companion that expands on the material and tailors it to your situation.

A printed book has limits in length and depth. Living Book Technology™ does not. Over time, readers will be able to explore extended examples, deeper explanations, additional prompts, and new perspectives that build on the core text.

The best way to prepare for Living Book Technology™ is by reading this work carefully and writing notes and questions along the way. Those questions and ideas are meant to become the starting point for a deeper conversation—one that begins after you turn the last page of the book. At that point, the work is designed to evolve from a manual—words on a page—into a coach and consultant.

Instead of simply reading a book and hoping to apply the lessons or concepts from it, Living Book Technology™ is built to help readers apply those lessons with guidance, context, and personalization.

This matters because traditional books deliver information, but Living Book Technology™ is designed to bring that information to life through interaction and adaptive support. It creates a new category of reading where a book becomes a coach, a companion, and a dynamic learning system built from the actual content of the work itself.

This title is the first book built for the platform. Readers will be invited to access Living Book Technology™ in phases as the system becomes available. Many future books, authors, and publishing projects will build on the same foundation. You are holding the starting point of a new chapter in publishing—the first book designed to become a living system.

ACKNOWLEDGEMENTS

This book was not written alone. Every chapter carries the fingerprints of the people, places, and crucibles that shaped me.

To my parents, Barry and Reagen: thank you for giving me both love of music and a sense of grit. To my mom, who sacrificed endlessly and modeled resilience every single day. To My dad, who inspired me to pick up the drums; who sacrificed part of his own music career to provide for our family; who passed down both creativity as well as entrepreneurial spirit.

To my sister Chelsea: who's shown me what it looks like to be the best mom ever. To my "Nice Niece" McKayla: this book is dedicated to you.

To Graysen Harnwel: my longtime business partner, brother, friend, and "Rich Bro." Thank you for your vision and strategy, for teaching me to see ten years ahead when I could only see ten feet. From late-night talks to building FlashPants, you've been more than a partner. You've been my brother from another mother.

To my mentors, teachers, and peers across industries—from drumline to real estate, from FlashPants to finance: thank you for sharpening me, challenging me, and showing me how skills transfer in ways I never could have imagined.

To Erin & Danny Williamson: thank you for being there for me through turbulent times and always having my back. Your presence is truly inspiring, and I love you both.

To Jamison Whitworth, D.C. and Emotional Healer: thank you for teaching me how the body stores old emotions and how to release them, while also modeling what it means to live with eternal optimism.

To Justin Egerer, D.C: thank you for being a steady example of grit, consistency, and respect for the natural order of things. And thank you for all the house calls and hockey games.

To Wilbur Salazar: Thank you for showing me how to truly absorb material through spaced repetition. You're a modern-day philosopher in every sense, and I'm grateful for the clarity and insight you bring to our conversations. And thank you as well for helping me with the proofreads and putting the final polish on this book.

To Ben Webber: Thank you for sitting down with me, talking honestly about life and strategy, and listening with the depth of someone who's been to the top. I'm truly grateful. And thank you for revealing the blind spot I somehow missed — that owning supercars and hypercars isn't an indulgence to justify, but a joy I'm allowed to fully step into. Apparently my subconscious was limiting horsepower.

To Dr. Samuel Jones, Leader of Wharton's MBA Career Management Office at the Wharton School of Business: Thank you for helping me compile, edit, and rebuild my résumé a few years after leaving real estate, during a period when I was actively rebuilding my identity and learning how to present myself as marketable to the professional world. I was disillusioned, but still hopeful—a job candidate more than a decade before earning my MBA, or any degree for that matter. Your guidance mattered more than you'll probably ever know.

To Dana Potter, founder of Pinnacle Estate Properties, Inc.: thank you for loaning me $250 back in 2005 so I could get my cavities filled while I was waiting for my first listing in escrow to close and was completely broke. I'll never forget that. And thank you for always reminding me, "We're not in the real estate business… we're in the lead generation business." That phrase has stuck with me, and I've carried and adapted it as I've moved into other industries where it still rings true.

To the students I've had the privilege of teaching—and those I continue to teach today: you gave me purpose. Your questions, breakthroughs, and struggles shaped this framework as much as my own experiences did.

And to Georgie, my dog from 1997 to 2013, forever in my heart.

To you, the reader holding this book: thank you for trusting me to guide you. My hope is that these lessons become tools you use, not just stories you consume. May you take them, stack them, and build something greater than you ever thought possible.

Above all, I want to thank God for the gift of life itself, for the unseen hand in every crucible, and for making all things possible.

TABLE OF CONTENTS

INTRODUCTION
THE FIRST STAGE

I'm 43 years old, and I've never had a "real" job.

Not because I'm a rich kid. Not because I wasn't ready to work. And definitely not because I had some master plan on day one.

I delivered pizzas at 30 and knocked on 7,000 doors trying to sell real estate in the middle of the worst housing collapse in decades. I've run around in red dolphin shorts and a fake mustache in front of millions of viewers on TV. I've taught people about crypto, options, stocks, forex and futures in hotel conference rooms. Built multiple revenue streams by applying the same core skills (sales, systems, and relationship building) across completely different industries.

Looking at that list, you probably think one of two things: either I'm lying, or I can't commit.

Both are totally wrong.

What you might not see is the through line. The skills that were transferred from one level to the next, like how getting rejected at 6,999 doors set me up precisely to land our first band's gig. Or how learning to feel the energy of a crowd prepared me to read a room of financial traders who were not getting the results they wanted out of the markets. Or how studying breathwork and energy healing made me a more effective business partner and leader.

You don't fall into a series of careers. You build them. One skill at a time.

The Trap Most People Never Escape

Here's what no one wants to admit: most people are stuck in what I call the single skill trap.

They went to school for something. Got good at it, maybe even great at it. Then life happened—the industry changes, the economy collapses, or the company downsizes. Suddenly, the one thing they have built isn't enough.

So what do most people do? They scramble back to the exact same spot they were before, as if the disruption was just a detour. But, as you will learn, crises and calamities are also often an opportunity: a call to level up.

That's something the self-help industry won't share. They'll tell you to "find your passion" like it's buried treasure. Or "follow your dreams" as if dreams pay the mortgage. The worst ones promise you can reinvent yourself in a weekend with enough positive thinking and a Pinterest board.

Total garbage.

Real reinvention doesn't come from discovering yourself. It comes from creating yourself.

Crisis by crisis. Skill by skill. Stack by stack.

Why You Should Listen to Me

I'm not a life coach. I never earned a degree in psychology, never authored a book (before this one), or gave a TED talk. I do have an MBA, but that's not what qualifies me to write this book.

What I do have is experience. I have been through the grind—and then some.

Our band, FlashPants.com, isn't some weekend cover band. We became the most booked '80s entertainment act in California. Multiple identical casts are playing in different cities at the same time. Corporate clients hire us for their biggest events. We've even won *The Gong Show*'s season finale on ABC in front of *three million viewers*.

You don't stumble into that by accident.

When COVID wiped out the entertainment industry in March 2020, I didn't panic. I took everything I'd learned, sales from booking shows, systems from building the band, stage presence from thousands of performances, and focused it on financial education. Within months, I was running trading classes, teaching everyday people about the markets.

Across every career transition, I've used the same foundational skills to solve problems in totally different industries. Booking entertainment. Teaching trading. Helping companies fix broken systems. None of this came from lucky breaks or knowing the right people. It came from learning how to mine transferable skills from every experience—especially the painful ones.

What Really Works

Every experience teaches you something worthwhile… if you're paying attention.

After leaving real estate, I had to learn how to be especially resourceful, mentally tough, and lean. Actually, I had a bit more than just a backpack: I had the car I was sleeping in. Those same skills reappeared later when I had to bootstrap FlashPants without capital.

When I trained for months in breathwork and energy healing, I had no idea what it would amount to. What I didn't realize was that I was cultivating empathy, presence, and the ability to read people. Those lessons made me a stronger bandleader, teacher, business partner, and friend.

While knocking on a total of 7,000 doors to get my first listing, I wasn't just learning real estate. I was developing grit, emotional control, pattern recognition, and sales—principles that apply in any business.

Most people see these as random chapters in a chaotic life. I see them as connected lessons in a deliberate education I didn't even know I was getting. The most valuable lesson was realizing that these experiences each held training opportunities and lessons, ripe for the picking.

This book isn't about a "follow your passion" fantasy. It's about creating a life that grows stronger under pressure instead of breaking under it. It's about learning to fashion those experiences (that may feel like a hodgepodge of skills and interests) into something that makes you unstoppable.

Inside, you'll discover my four-step diagnostic system for pinpointing exactly where you are today. Whether you're in full crisis mode, managing long-term depletion, stuck in stagnation, or poised for your next breakthrough, each stage demands a different strategy.

You'll learn how to recognize skills you already have but don't think of as skills. Most people are sitting on valuable, transferable abilities they've never considered using.

You'll see how skills actually compound. Foundational abilities blend into mid-range competencies, which develop into top-tier skills that create exponential possibilities. This isn't motivational fluff. It's the exact roadmap I've used to build everything.

You'll find real-world examples of how unrelated abilities transfer into new domains. How drumming rhythm translates into business timing. Why every relationship improves with sales training. How the healing arts shape leadership presence.

You'll gain practical roadmaps for combining skills into stacks most people overlook. Top performers in any field are simply skill stackers who discovered the right combinations.

Most of all, you'll stop waiting for permission to reinvent yourself.

Using the QR Codes

You'll notice there aren't any photos printed in this book. That's intentional. I love non-fiction books, but I also know this: the shorter the page count, the higher the odds I will actually finish them. Chances are, you feel the same. That's why I designed this book to be as efficient as possible with the real estate inside these pages, so you can move fast, get the ideas, and save time.

But if you want to dig deeper into the content, there are photos, videos, templates, and audio for you. I've taken care of putting QR codes for you to access that bonus content. Scan them with your camera app (or any QR code scanner on your phone) and you'll unlock extras like:

- Photos of the key events mentioned
- Videos that drop you right into the scene
- Audio clips from performances, talks, or behind the curtain
- Charts and templates that expand on key concepts

Think of these like DVD bonus features—optional, never required. The book stands on its own, but the codes let you step deeper into the story if time and curiosity permit.

This way, you get the best of both worlds: a book that's lean and efficient, plus the ability to explore more whenever you want.

CHAPTER 1
TRIAGE YOUR LIFE

*Things that matter most must never be
at the mercy of things that matter least.*
—*Johann Wolfgang von Goethe*

David's laptop mocked him. The cursor blinked on a blank resignation email he'd been trying, and failing, to write for three weeks. Every attempt ended the same: his brain spiraling into chaos.

The job was crushing him. Sixty-hour weeks. A boss who changed priorities daily. Projects that never went anywhere. His relationship with Abigail was unraveling. His back screamed from endless hours hunched over spreadsheets. Stress eating had packed fifteen pounds on his frame, and the gym felt like a distant memory.

Yet quitting seemed impossible. The paycheck was steady. His parents kept asking when he'd finally get promoted. And the darker question haunted him: what if nothing better was out there?

"Dude, you look awful," Jake said, sliding into the cafe booth. "Still stuck on that job situation?"

David rubbed his temples. "Everything's collapsing. Work's a disaster, Abigail and I barely talk. I feel like trash, and I don't even know what I want in life. I can't fix all of it."

Jake leaned back, calm. "Remember when I tried to remodel my entire house in one week? You told me not everything imperfect is an emergency."

"That's different."

"Is it?" Jake pulled out his pen and sketched a quick diagram on a napkin. "My brother's business coach showed him this. There are four levels of life crisis. Most people treat level twos like level ones."

He labeled them:

- *Level one: True emergency. You're about to lose everything.*
- *Level two: Unsustainable but manageable. You're burning out, but not dying.*

- *Level three: Stagnant but safe. Stable, but stale.*
- *Level four: Optimization mode. You're fine, just tuning.*

"The trick," Jake said, "is diagnosing where you really are. Then matching your response to the level instead of panicking."

David studied the napkin. "So what level am I at?"

"Are you about to lose your apartment or end up in the hospital if you don't act right now?"

"No, but—"

"Then it's not level one. How about work? How many hours are you working?"

"Too many," David admitted. "I can't keep this up. The headaches are constant."

"Then you're at level two, serious depletion. That calls for strategy, not panic. You don't need to quit your job tomorrow, fix your relationship, and hit the gym all at once. Just take pressure off one area so you have energy for the others."

"But which one do I start with?"

"Which one is causing you the most pain?"

David didn't have to think long. The job. It poisoned his patience with Abigail, killed his motivation to work out, and left him no mental space to think about his future.

"The job," he said.

"Exactly. So don't blow it up with no plan. Start small. Leave at six. Stop checking email at night. Use the freed-up energy to plan your next move."

Something loosened in David's chest. "That actually feels doable."

Jake nodded. "You've been treating stagnation like a crisis and burning yourself out trying to fix everything at once. Real triage means handling what's most pressing first—then working outward."

*
**

Like David, you probably have multiple fires competing for your attention. Here's the good news: this chapter will show you how to diagnose your real situation, separate urgent from optional, and match your response to reality, not to your anxiety. You'll stop trying to fix everything at once and instead learn how to triage like a pro, taking the right step at the right time to build momentum.

What Is Triage?

Nobody drifts into a new life. Reinvention starts in the fire, inside a crucible.

A crucible is built to withstand heat. You don't put something in a crucible to protect it. You put it there to transform it: to melt away what's false, to leave behind what's real, and to forge something stronger. That's what a crisis does in our lives. That's what rock bottom does. Betrayal, bankruptcy, heartbreak, illness, failure—they're all crucibles.

But here's what most people miss: not all crucibles are the same. Some demand an immediate response; others require strategy. Some crucibles can be handled with steady, incremental action. Others are opportunities for growth in disguise. The danger is that most people treat *every* problem like a five-alarm fire. They panic over stagnation. They overanalyze true emergencies. They waste energy on the wrong battles while the real ones bleed out.

Your life doesn't need panic. It needs triage.

The Four Stages of a Life Crisis — Your Survival Map

Every crisis isn't created equal. Over the years, I've learned every tough situation falls into one of four categories—and each demands a completely different response. Misjudge the level, and you'll waste energy—panicking over inconveniences or sleepwalking through true emergencies.

Level 1: 911 – Total System Failure

This is the red zone. Not just hard, but impossible.

For me, that was my exodus from real estate. I was deep in the business at an incredibly difficult time. The market was in turmoil, and everyone was trying to navigate uncertainty the best they could. I could have stayed and leaned into short sales and foreclosures like many agents did to survive. A lot of good people found ways to adapt.

But I was burned out. I didn't yet have the self-awareness or the communication skills to ask for support, set boundaries, or articulate what I was struggling with. The pressure of the market, combined with my own internal misalignment, became too much. I was watching families sign complex loans they didn't fully understand, and while many professionals were doing their best in a chaotic system, I felt increasingly uneasy. It wasn't that the entire industry was corrupt—it was that I was out of alignment with where I was, who I was becoming, and what I was equipped to handle at the time.

So I left. Not because real estate was inherently wrong, but because I wasn't right within it anymore.

I was broke, saddled with debt, and without any sort of backup plan. Still, I knew one thing: staying meant becoming someone I didn't respect. So leaving the industry was an easy choice for my soul, but my pocketbook suffered badly.

That's **911 territory.** The system you're in isn't just broken. It's toxic.

911 Emergency signs:

- Your situation violates core values.
- Continuing means more damage than stopping.
- You're staring at total financial, physical, or emotional collapse.
- The system itself is corrupt.

Response: Stop the bleeding. Exit first. Survive. Forget optimization until you're not drowning.

Level 2: Rush to ER — Serious but Beatable

This is where you're running, but at a pace that'll break you if you keep going. You're burning energy faster than it can be replaced.

That was me during the pandemic. FlashPants went from 200+ shows a year to zero overnight. No venues. No corporate gigs. No weddings. Entertainment was dead.

However, unlike 2008, I had skills, systems, and income streams in place. I wasn't going to lose my home or go hungry. Still, I was grinding 16-hour days: learning to trade, building educational content, and keeping the band's infrastructure alive for whenever the world reopened.

Manageable. But not sustainable.

Drive to ER signs:

- Chronic overwork can damage your health or relationships.
- Living in firefighting mode, never building anything new.
- Short-term survival is working, but the long-term is unsustainable.
- You're exhausted, but not in immediate danger.

Response: Strategic intervention. Cut pressure, create space, and move toward something better. Survival pales in comparison to preventing collapse.

Silent Depletion and Dopamine Addiction

One of the most common ways people deplete themselves is by starting their day inundated by the world. You know the drill: eyes barely open, phone in hand, notifications crashing into your nervous system before your feet hit the floor. It feels normal now, but think back: twenty years ago, would you have sprinted to your mailbox at 6 A.M. to rip open every piece of mail before brushing your teeth?

Of course not. You would have eased into the day—coffee, shower, maybe some quiet—then dealt with the world.

When you grab the phone first thing, it may feel like you're innocently catching up on emails or news feeds. In reality, you're inviting the unfiltered chaos of the world into your head, before you've had a chance to center yourself. That's not preparation. It's destabilizing.

Here's the truth: the morning is your only window to set the tone for the day before the world starts tugging at you. Protect it. Wake up naturally. Meditate, pray, journal, or just sit in silence. Get grounded first. Then—and only then—turn your phone off silent and let the world trickle in.

Because the second you "ping" back online, you've sent the signal. Think about *The Matrix*, when the crew powered up their radar underground. The sentinels swarmed it instantly. That's what happens when you light up your notifications. You've told the world exactly where to find you, and it will.

If you want out of depletion mode, start here. Don't begin the day with inundation. Begin with intention.

Level 3: Urgent Care – Stagnation to Momentum

At this Level, you're safe, but stuck. You aren't in danger, but you are not growing either.

That was me after leaving real estate, before FlashPants was born. Delivering pizzas. Playing drums in random bands. Paying bills. Surviving, not thriving.

The basics were covered. I wasn't broke or homeless. But I wasn't building anything meaningful. Life was flat.

Urgent Care signs:

- Needs met, but boredom creeping in

- Going through motions without real engagement

- You know you could do more, but don't know what

- Stable, but uninspired

Response: Incremental progress. Experiment. Explore new skills. Push edges with minimal risk. This is prime time for low-pressure growth.

Level 4: Wellness Check – Primed for Growth

This is optimization mode. Life is steady. Systems are working. You're not scrambling to survive. You're positioned to expand.

This is where I am today. FlashPants is thriving with multiple casts. Teaching trading is rewarding and profitable. Consulting projects align with my strengths. Health is good. Relationships are strong. And this book? It shows us that legacy matters more than mere survival.

Wellness Check signs:

- Needs met consistently without stress

- Engaged in projects that matter

- Relationships energize instead of drain

- Ready to expand, give back, or take on bigger challenges

Response: Strategic growth. Take bold risks. Build legacy projects. Teach, mentor, and multiply impact.

The key is recognizing the level you're actually in, so you can stop overreacting to stagnation and stop underestimating real threats.

The Skills Triage

Most people never reinvent their lives because they misdiagnose the level they're actually in. They treat Level Three stagnation like a Level One emergency, turning boredom into drama. Or worse, they treat a Level One collapse like Level Three, trying to "optimize" a system that's already dead. Both approaches waste energy and keep them stuck.

When you learn to analyze your situation correctly, you build four transferable skills that apply everywhere:

- **Crisis Recognition** – Knowing the difference between discomfort and a true emergency. Most "crises" are really just Level 3 stagnation dressed up as panic.

- **Real Analysis** – Facts over feelings. The 2008 financial crisis wiped out approximately $16 trillion in U.S. household net worth, including $7 trillion in real estate value and $8 trillion in stock market capitalization. In 2009, the real estate market had bottomed out after so many had lost so much. That wasn't an emotional judgment—it was reality. Whether I felt bad about leaving a "good" career was irrelevant.

- **Strategic Thinking** – Matching the right response to the right situation. You don't call 911 for a paper cut, and you don't try a Band-Aid when an artery's blown.

- **Self-Awareness** – Seeing your situation without denial or drama. Most people either exaggerate small problems or downplay real ones.

These four skills become the backbone of every major decision you'll make for the rest of your life.

How Triage Transfers to Everything

This framework isn't just for personal crises. It applies everywhere—business, relationships, career, even money. Once you see the four levels, you start seeing them in every area of life.

Business

A business can be broken at the foundation (Level 1), running unsustainably (Level 2), stuck in a flat-but-stable plateau (Level 3), or primed for strategic expansion (Level 4).

For example, a startup with a flawed product is in a 911 emergency—no marketing tweak fixes that. But a restaurant with slow Tuesdays isn't in crisis; that's simple Level 3 stagnation, not existential collapse.

Relationships

The same logic applies to people. Some relationships are toxic at the core (Level

1), some are strained and wearing you down (Level 2), some are comfortable but stagnant (Level 3), and some are thriving (Level 4).

Physical abuse is a Level 1 crisis. A couple stuck in a predictable routine? That's Level 3. A draining friendship that's chipping away at your energy? Level 2.

Career

Your job can fall into any of the four levels too. If the role itself is disappearing or damaging your health, that's Level 1. If you're burning out under chronic stress, that's Level 2. Bored but stable? Level 3. Supported and growing? Level 4.

A job being automated away is true 911 territory. A well-paid but uninspiring role is just stagnation. An abusive boss? Serious depletion—Level 2.

Once you understand the four levels, you stop treating every problem the same. You match the response to the situation.

Chapter 1 Activity: Diagnosing Your Situation

Step 1: Select Your Focus

Which area of life needs the most attention right now?

- Career/Professional
- Health/Physical
- Relationships/Family
- Financial
- Purpose/Meaning

Step 2: Know Your Level

Which level matches your situation?

- **911:** Total breakdown. Current path is impossible. Immediate intervention required.

- **ER:** Manageable but unsustainable. Chronic stress. You're functional but headed for collapse.

- **Urgent Care:** Stable but stagnant. Safe but dull. Ready for incremental progress.

- **Wellness Check:** Functioning well. Time to optimize, expand, or grow strategically.

Step 3: Match Your Response to Your Level

- **911:** What's the absolute minimum you can do to stop the bleeding? Survival first, optimization later.

- **ER:** What one change would cut pressure by 50%? Prioritize sustainability, not perfection.

- **Urgent Care:** What's one small experiment you can run this week to build momentum?

- **Wellness:** What growth play aligns with your current strengths?

Your life isn't random. It's diagnosable. And once diagnosed, it's actionable.

Wrapping It Up

Like David at the start of this chapter, you may feel pulled in a dozen directions at once. But here's the truth: you can't stack skills if you don't know which ones you need right now. You can't make tactical choices if you don't know your position on the map. Skip this step, and you'll use the wrong tool on the wrong problem, trying to optimize a collapse or treating stagnation like a five-alarm fire. Wrong diagnosis, wrong action, wrong outcome.

Before you layer on relationships, opportunities, money, or new skills, you need clarity. Where are you, really?

That's what this chapter gave you: a four-level triage system to cut through noise and drama. Most situations fall into one of four categories—emergency, depletion, stagnation, optimization.

By diagnosing your actual level and committing to address just one area first, you stop wasting energy in the wrong direction and start creating traction where it counts.

Now comes the next question: what skills do you already have to work with? Most people underestimate their assets. They assume they're starting from zero when in reality they're carrying a toolkit of skills, experiences, and patterns they've never fully acknowledged.

The next chapter will change that. We're going to take inventory, uncovering the dormant abilities, transferable experiences, and hidden assets you already own. Because once you see the arsenal at your disposal, reinvention stops being overwhelming and starts being strategic.

CHAPTER 2

TAKING STOCK
OF YOUR SKILLS

*You have within you, right now, everything you need to deal with
whatever the world can throw at you.*

—Brian Tracy

Leah sat across from the interview panel and tried to keep her hands still.
"We're looking for someone who can manage competing priorities," the man
at the end of the table said. "Tell us about a time when different commitments
competed for your attention."

Leah's mind went blank. She thought of color-coded calendars, to-do lists,
alarms, parent-teacher meetings. None of it sounded right. She talked about a
school fundraiser she'd helped with years ago. Almost as soon as she spoke, she
could hear how small it sounded. She felt silly using her private life in an interview.

They thanked her. She thanked them. In the parking lot, she sat in her
car, watching people pass with lanyards and coffee cups, and felt the familiar
weight settle in her chest. Eight years at home, and she still didn't know how to
explain herself.

That evening, her phone rang while she was chopping onions. The pediatri-
cian's office. Her youngest had spiked a fever at school. At the same moment, her
oldest started shouting from the living room—over a history project meltdown—
and the middle one announced he needed a poster board *tonight*.

Leah turned down the stove. She asked the office to hold and separated the
kids. She recalculated dinner. She checked the calendar, texted another parent,
found a poster board in the hall closet, and packed a bag for the doctor—all
without raising her voice. The next morning was hardly different. Leah began by
feeding the hungry, giving drink to the thirsty, and getting them ready for school.

By the time she locked the front door behind them, she was already in full
stride. She didn't think of it as skill. She thought of it as Tuesday.

That interview question surfaced again in her mind.

Manage competing priorities.

She almost laughed. Not because it was funny, but because she finally understood why, in a panic, she used her experience as a stay-at-home mom. Her skills were not just those that fit neatly on a resume. They were those that made her a great mother, parent, family receptionist, PTA board member, and spouse. What made Leah an asset was Leah.

Her phone rang. It was the interviewer calling. She got the job.

*
**

To be frank, most people are just like Leah: sitting on a mountain of skills they dismiss as "just what I had to do." But skills are skills, whether you learned them in a boardroom, a garage, or a kitchen. And unless you recognize them, you'll keep undervaluing yourself.

Burn the Ships

When I walked away from real estate in 2009, I felt like I was starting from zero.

The market had collapsed, and the uncertainty shook everything. It was a painful season for a lot of good professionals. For me, it forced deeper questions about alignment, purpose, and who I was becoming. I didn't have the language for it at the time, but I knew I couldn't continue the way I had been. I also knew I didn't want to trade one version of misalignment for another—sitting in an office under fluorescent lighting, trying to force myself into a mold that didn't fit. So I left. No plan B. No backup. Just a clean break.

On paper, my skills suddenly felt hard to translate. How do you explain a season of selling homes during one of the most volatile periods in housing history? How do you frame that experience when you're questioning your own direction? I didn't yet understand how to articulate the transferable skills I'd built—negotiation, persistence, marketing, resilience. All I could see was what wasn't working.

So it felt like I had nothing.

I was dead wrong.

It took me years to see it: my skills grew more visible after I chose to leave. I hadn't just been selling homes; I'd been sharpening negotiation, building client relationships, solving messy problems, and managing pressure. I was blind to my own capabilities.

Untapped Gold

This is the trap: most people massively underestimate what they bring to the table.

They believe skills only count if they come with a certificate, a degree, or a job title. They dismiss lived experiences as survival, not strategy. They fail to realize that every role, paid or unpaid, is a laboratory for building transferable skills.

When I knocked on 7,000 doors chasing my first real estate listing, I thought I was just drowning in rejection. In reality, I was building grit, emotional control, pattern recognition, and sales fundamentals I still rely on today.

When I trained in breathwork, I thought I was just helping people calm down. I didn't realize I was building empathy, presence, and adaptability. These are traits that later made me a stronger bandleader, teacher, and business partner.

When I was scaling FlashPants from a group of weekend warriors into multiple casts across California and Arizona, I thought I was just holding the chaos together. In truth, I was learning systems thinking, leadership, and process design under fire.

The skills were always there; I just didn't know how to name them.

And the bottom line is: if you can't name your skills, you can't cash in on them.

Blind To Bounty

When I left real estate, here's the contrast between what I thought I had and what I truly carried forward:

What I thought I had:

- experience selling houses

- awareness of local market conditions

- a list of past clients

- some sales training

What I really had:
- **Grit** – I'd knocked on 7,000 doors and kept going after 6,999 rejections.

- **Emotional regulation** – I could absorb a *no* without collapsing.

- **Pattern recognition** – I learned to tell which conversations had potential and which were dead ends.

- **Relationship building** – I knew how to approach strangers and win trust quickly.

- **Systems thinking** – I could manage complex transactions with dozens of moving parts.
- **Persistence** – I sustained effort without immediate reward.
- **Flexibility** – I adapted my style to what actually worked.

That gap between the two lists is massive. One perspective frames you as unemployed; the other frames you as competent and valuable. What we're really talking about here is leverage, not just a mindset shift.

The Skill Matrix

To make this practical, I break skills into three levels: raw, mid-tier, and premium. This structure helps you identify what you already possess. And, more importantly, how to combine them for maximum leverage.

Raw Skills (Basic)

These are the fundamentals. Everyone has them in some form, but most people don't recognize their value. They transfer into any environment.

From my real estate grind:

- Courage – Knocking on strangers' doors.
- Listening – Catching what people actually needed.
- Persistence – Pushing forward when results didn't come right away.
- Curiosity – Asking instead of assuming.
- Resilience – Rebounding from rejection without losing steam.

Common raw skills most people overlook:

- Problem-solving
- Communication
- Time management
- Learning ability
- Stress tolerance
- Attention to detail
- Teamwork

These might seem basic, but they're the foundation. Someone with strong raw skills can learn mid-tier skills fast. Without them, no amount of training sticks.

The Six Flags Crucible

My first real job was the summer before 11th grade, in 1998. I landed what I thought was the dream gig at the time: ride operator at Six Flags Magic Mountain in Santa Clarita.

As a kid, I'd always wanted to push buttons on elevators, roller coasters—pretty much anything mechanical. At sixteen, I finally got paid to do it. I was assigned to Area 5, Pirates Cove, which meant running three rides: the Swashbuckler (towering swings that rose and fell), the Buccaneer (a giant pirate ship), and the Jolly Roger (a flat ride that spun people silly).

Six Flags had manuals and systems for everything from ride operation, safety checks, and even how to clean up vomit. Each shift started with wardrobe issuing us themed costumes. I passed the exams for all three rides and became "area certified." For a teenager, it felt like middle management.

But theory didn't prepare me for chaos. One night there were wide-scale riots. Fights broke out, guests smashed property, and us employees scrambled to close merchandise stands before they were looted. Security was nowhere. We had to improvise in real-time while the park remained open. That night drilled into me the importance of situational awareness, composure under pressure, and adapting fast when systems fall apart.

We survived unscathed, but the lessons stuck.

Later, I leveled up to the big ride: Colossus, the massive wooden coaster built from eight million feet of lumber. Running Colossus was precision work. Each operator had to give a thumbs-up confirming every lap bar before dispatching a train. We added our own flair with the mic: "Push down, pull up, exit to your right, and enjoy your stay at Six Flags… Disneyland." Guests would look around, confused.

We also developed codes. "Five ten, one two" meant someone was stuck in train one, seat two. But we had our own version: "Ten five, one two" meant a cute girl was sitting in that spot. Teenagers with microphones always find ways to keep it fun.

Some moments weren't funny. One night, a train stalled at the very top of the lift hill. They strapped a helmet and flashlight on me and told me to climb up and calm the passengers. It was the longest hike of my life. Just as I reached them, the system rebooted, and the train plunged. My legs were toast for two days after that climb.

Then there were crew rides. After the park closed, mechanics had to cycle the trains to park them overnight, and they'd let staff hop in. It was the ultimate perk—but we made it reckless. Sometimes we'd ride without lap bars, gripping a tiny cutout under the seats. One night, my coworker Arbel lost his grip and literally flew out of his seat on the first drop until we pulled him back in. Add to that the mechanics leaving the drive tires running (meant for empty trains) while we were fully loaded, and the coaster tore through at warp speed, sparks flying off the upstop wheels. It was insane. I'm sure crew rides don't exist anymore for good reason.

Looking back, Six Flags wasn't just a teenage job. It was my first crucible in systems, rules, teamwork, and improvisation. I learned that even the simplest "button-pushing" role is really about process discipline, people management, and quick thinking when things go sideways. Those were raw skills (situational awareness, communication, and composure under pressure) that would show up again and again in every future stack.

The eBay Gold Rush: Lovejoy Collectibles

My second job came right after high school, in 2000, when my best friend Zach's dad Gary launched an eBay business called Lovejoy Collectibles out of his warehouse in Simi Valley. Back then, eBay was still the Wild West: if you had inventory, you could move it fast and make serious money.

Gary dedicated a room in his warehouse just for the operation, and I helped set it up. I wasn't a tech wizard, but I knew enough about computers to wire towers, connect everything to the internet, and get the office network running, which felt like a big deal at the time. We had a legit setup: a full packing and shipping station, a commercial peanut dispenser, boxes stacked by size, and tape guns ready to go.

I got an unexpected education in antiques and collectibles: Fenton glass, Royal Doulton figurines, hobnail patterns, sports memorabilia, Department 56 Christmas villages, even the "Pinky and Blue Boy" portraits. My responsibilities touched everything—photographing and listing items, packing orders, handling customer service, and learning the quirks of buyers in niche markets.

One night I told my first girlfriend, "Gary thinks I might be able to make $70,000 if we keep this up." She rolled her eyes—it sounded crazy for an 18-year-old. But perspective is everything. Adjusted for inflation, that $70,000 in 2000 would be around $125,000 in 2025. I didn't hit that number selling antiques, but a few years later, I eclipsed it in real estate. That moment taught me two things: first, perspective matters; second, entrepreneurship could scale far beyond hourly labor if you built systems.

Lovejoy was my crash course in small business. I learned customer service, inventory management, logistics, and operations, all by accident. More importantly, it showed me that business is less about luck and more about building systems that let value flow. That lesson would stick.

Mid-Tier Skills (Developed)

These come through practice, training, or experience. They're more specialized than raw skills, but still transferable across contexts.

From my journey:

- Sales – Leading people to decisions.

- Public speaking – Communicating clearly to groups.

- Project management – Juggling multiple tasks and deadlines.

- Coaching – Helping others perform better.

- Design thinking – Solving problems through system design.

- Leadership – Inspiring and organizing teams.

Mid-tier skills are the resume items, the things people talk about in interviews. But they're still just building blocks: useful, but not yet explosive.

Premium Skills (Stacked Combinations)

This is where real leverage appears. Premium skills are combinations of raw and mid-tier abilities that multiply each other instead of just adding up.

From my career:

- **Entrepreneurship**: Vision + risk tolerance + systems thinking + sales + leadership.

- **Teaching**: Communication + empathy + subject matter expertise + performance + coaching.

- **Entertainment leadership**: Stage presence + team management + creative vision + business systems.

Few people ever think in terms of synergy. They learn skills in isolation, never asking how to combine them into rare stacks. But it's in the combinations where exponential opportunities hide.

The question isn't just *what skills do you have?* It's *how do you combine them into something no one else can replicate?*

The Skills I Never Knew I Had

The biggest breakthrough in my own skill inventory came when I realized I'd been sitting on abilities I never intentionally set out to learn. They weren't obvious at the time, but they became some of my most valuable professional assets.

- **Stage presence** – Years of performing in bands weren't just "being a musician." They trained me to stay calm under pressure, read an audience, and adjust my delivery in real time. Confidence, timing, and energy awareness. These are skills that later made every presentation, meeting, and teaching opportunity more powerful.

- **Crisis management** – Surviving the real estate collapse, sleeping in my car, and rebuilding from scratch wasn't just "getting through a rough patch." It was learning antifragility: the ability to get stronger under pressure instead of breaking down.

- **Culture bridging** – Working with real estate clients from all walks of life, performing FlashPants shows for every demographic imaginable, and teaching diverse groups of students in trading education wasn't just "being friendly." It was learning how to bridge gaps, make anyone feel heard, and connect across differences—a rare skill that translates everywhere.

- **Systems building** Scaling FlashPants from chaos into a repeatable business model wasn't just "getting organized." It was learning how to design processes that run without me—creating systems that multiply impact instead of draining me.

These weren't skills I set out to collect. They emerged from lived experience. And yet, they turned out to be some of the most bankable tools in my professional arsenal.

How Skill Recognition Transfers to Everything

Once you learn to recognize your skills, every transition gets easier because you stop underselling yourself and start reframing your value.

Job Interviews

Don't just list duties. Translate them into transferable assets.

- Instead of: "I ran restaurant operations."
  Say: "I mastered crisis management, team coordination, and pressure performance optimization."

- Instead of: "I supervised 12 people."
  Say: "I developed conflict resolution skills, learned to motivate different personalities, and created systems for consistent output."

- Instead of: "I dealt with customer complaints."
  Say: "I built emotional control, learned de-escalation, and developed pattern recognition to prevent recurring issues."

Career Change

The same rule applies: carry skills forward.

- My drumming career didn't look relevant to business until I realized timing, rhythm, and performance map directly to teaching and leadership.

- A veteran might realize logistics coordination, pressure-tested team leadership, and structured problem-solving translate into corporate project management.

- A former restaurant server can reframe multitasking, emotional regulation, and reading customer needs as the exact skills needed for client success roles in tech.

- A librarian can shift into UX design by recognizing that organizing information, guiding research, and helping people find what they need are the same core abilities in a new context.

The power is in the reframe. Once you can name and claim your hidden skills, you stop looking like someone starting from zero and start looking like someone with a track record of proven, transferable assets.

Building Relationships

When you understand your people skills, you gain leverage. You can double down on strengths and deliberately shore up weaknesses.

For me, recognizing that I was strong at reading energy but weaker in direct communication changed everything. It reshaped how I approached business partnerships, friendships, and even conflict.

It works the same for you:

- If you're a great listener but weak on boundaries, you lean on empathy while developing assertiveness.

- If you're a big-picture thinker who misses details, you find a partner who thrives on precision to balance you out.

- If you're strong in written communication but stumble in verbal conflict, you prepare your words in advance or handle sensitive topics in writing.

The point: once you know yourself, you can design interactions and partnerships that play to your strengths while neutralizing your blind spots.

Entrepreneurship

Skill recognition doesn't just strengthen relationships, it also uncovers business opportunities that fit you like a glove.

My current consulting practice exists because I combined marketing expertise, systems thinking, and problem-solving into tailored solutions businesses actually needed.

Visit our website: YPARfirm.com

The same applies to you:

- A graphic designer with visual talent + a psychology degree + social media savvy can dominate the mental health marketing niche.

- A physical therapist with injury-prevention expertise + systems knowledge + teaching skills can create corporate wellness programs that cut workers' comp claims.

- An accountant with stage experience can turn financial education into engaging workshops, standing out in a sea of dull advisors.

When you learn to see combinations, you stop competing on commodity skills and start creating unique offerings only you can deliver.

Chapter 2 Activity: Your Skill Inventory Assessment

Time to find out what you're really working with. Most people skip this step and undersell themselves for years. Don't. This is where you discover your real arsenal.

Your task: Complete the five-step inventory below. Don't censor yourself. Write everything down, even the things you'd normally dismiss. Awareness requires articulation.

Step 1: Experience Audit

List all significant experiences from the last 10 years:

- Jobs (full-time, part-time, temp, freelance, volunteering)
- Serious hobbies or interests
- Challenges you overcame (personal, financial, health, professional)
- Projects you finished (work, personal, creative)
- Roles you played (parent, caregiver, organizer, teammate)

Don't filter. If it took effort, it counts.

Step 2: Recognition of Raw Skills

For each experience, ask yourself:

- What personal traits did I need to succeed?
- How did I handle stress, setbacks, or uncertainty?
- What specific skills did I use over and over again?
- Why did I ultimately succeed in that situation?

Step 3: Mid-Tier Skills Recognition

Go deeper. Identify the developed skills.

- Which abilities did I strengthen or refine?
- What do people consistently rely on me for?

- What do I do easily that others find difficult?

Step 4: Premium Skill Combinations

Now look for synergy.

- Which 3–4 skills do I naturally combine most often?
- What problems can I solve that most people can't?
- Where do my experiences overlap in unusual ways?
- What can I do that blends unrelated skills into something unique?

Step 5: Revealing Concealed Assets

This is where the gold often hides.

- What am I good at "by accident"?
- What natural strengths do I overlook because they come easily?
- What do I do that surprises people but feels effortless?
- What hard situations forced me to develop skills I now take for granted?

Complete this inventory, and you'll see what you're actually carrying. Not theory. Not wishful thinking. Real, transferable skills you can leverage today.

Wrapping It Up

Leah thought eight years of being "just a mom" was a gap in her résumé—until she saw it for what it was: high-level project management and crisis leadership. Chances are, you're sitting on the same kind of hidden capital. Skills you've minimized as "just what I had to do" are in fact transferable professional assets waiting to be named and leveraged.

This chapter gave you the process: a systematic inventory of raw foundational abilities, developed mid-tier skills, and premium combinations. The point is simple: you're not starting from zero. You're building on a proven base of abilities you've already demonstrated you can learn and apply.

Skill inventory is the foundation for everything that follows. You can't build strategically without knowing your starting assets. You can't identify money-making combinations without acknowledging the ingredients you already possess. Too many people sell themselves short for years because they never take stock.

They see themselves as beginners when in reality they're intermediates who simply haven't cashed in on their current assets.

This isn't about inflating yourself into something you're not. It's about seeing clearly what you've already built, so you can compound it strategically.

Now that you know what you're working with, it's time to move beyond inventory and into multiplication. The next chapter will reveal the **Skill Pyramid System**—how discrete skills combine into exponential leverage.

Your current skills are worth more than you think. Their full value is unlocked only when you learn how to stack them.

CHAPTER 3
THE SKILL PYRAMID –
HOW STACKING WORKS

Concentrate all your thoughts upon the work at hand. The sun's rays do not burn until brought to a focus.

—Alexander Graham Bell

Simon had been stuck as a project manager for three years, watching coworkers leapfrog past him at the computer firm. He'd applied in vain to senior roles at other organizations, but no one was biting. On paper, he was solid: reliable, well-liked, known as a problem solver. But in reality, his career had stalled.

"I'm good at my job," he told his mentor, Hannah, over lunch. "I hit deadlines. I keep teams happy. I handle problems before they blow up. But I'm not moving forward."

Hannah leaned in. "Those are a lot of skills. But what makes you *unique?*"

"Project management, I guess," Simon said. "That's my title. Keeping timelines, wrangling departments, making sure deliverables land."

Hannah reached into her purse and pulled out a notebook. "Break that down a little more. What else do you actually do?"

Simon sighed. "I see where the ball's going—stopping problems before they become serious. I translate between the technical teams and the business folks. Upper management trusts me to improvise solutions for the shipping and handling teams. And honestly? I've written half the operating procedures for the company at this point…"

Hannah smiled, scribbling as he spoke. When she turned the notebook around, Simon blinked.

Cross-department communication. Operating procedure development. Process optimization. International logistics management.

Simon thought for a moment. "I help companies avoid chaos. I see where breakdowns are coming and build systems to stop them before they hit. And

I translate between groups so complex processes become simple enough for everyone to follow."

Hannah nodded. "Exactly. That's not project management. That's operations strategy."

It clicked. He wasn't just organizing tasks, wrangling teams. He was streamlining how entire organizations functioned.

That single reframe changed everything. Simon stopped chasing "Senior Project Manager" postings and started applying for Operations Strategy and Business Process Improvement roles. Six months later, he landed a Director of Operational Excellence position—with a 40% salary increase.

*
**

Most people are like Simon. Sitting on a mountain of skills, focusing on what their titles or formal experience has taught them to value instead. But skills are skills, no matter where you got them—the boardroom, the kitchen, or the garage. Still, many people fail to look at themselves creatively, locking their skills behind a job title or degree. Yet until you recognize those skills, you'll keep selling yourself short.

This is the trap most people fall into: ignoring their skills because they did not earn them in the traditional way—on the job or in the classroom—or because they are not the best in that domain. It's what we might call the *Talladega Nights* trap. In the movie, NASCAR driver Ricky Bobby, played by Will Ferrell, repeats his mantra "if you ain't first, you're last." Meaning? Unless you're the best, you're not worth anything. But in the real world, plenty of second-best, fifth-best, even 1000th-best people succeed because of their unique combination of skills in other domains; it is their skillset that provides outsized value.

When I walked away from real estate in 2009, I felt like I was starting from zero.

The industry collapsed under a wave of excess and reckless incentives. Many good agents were caught in a system that had stretched too far. I had a clean conscience, but what I didn't have was a backup plan—or money. So I started looking for a new job. Unfortunately, my skills didn't translate the way I hoped. A real estate license in the middle of a housing crash wasn't exactly a golden ticket.

But that desperation gave me a fresh perspective. I realized that I was not just in the business of selling houses. I'd been generating leads, calling prospects, hearing rejections, overcoming rejections, sharpening my negotiation skills, building relationships, solving complex deals, handling pressure. All along I had built up a suite of skills that I was blind to.

The skill I thought I'd been developing was real estate. The skill stack I'd been cultivating was emotional—the grit to knock on 7,000 doors to get my first deal, the perseverance to knock day after day, the grace to hear countless noes and unkind words. Those skills were not on the test. They were earned on the streets. And in my case, it was the very last door of 7,000 that held my first deal. *The last will be first.*

Basic Skills

The first step in developing your skills is recognizing them. It sounds simple enough. In the Activity section at the end of this chapter, I've provided some handy resources for taking inventory of the skills you already possess. These kinds of skills are what I call Basic Skills—the skills we all have in some measure or another.

We can think of them as what most people call raw talent or instinct. Some people are naturally gifted with singing or dancing or calculating large numbers in their heads. But without cultivating these gifts, they remain largely untapped. In my real estate days, I learned that I had a natural talent for getting to know people quickly. Without practice and persistence, that skill would have remained middling or even withered on the vine.

Like most boys, I had the instinct to be like my Dad, who was a talented musician. He was a guitarist who'd jammed with Jimi Hendrix, hung out with Frank Zappa, riffed on the Merv Griffin show, and ripped up and down Sunset Strip in the 60s and 70s. I wanted to bond with him, so I took up drumming.

At first, I hated practicing alone. The drum set felt lonely. But being part of a drumline? That was different. The drumline meant accountability, community, shared goals. It wasn't just about me—it was about the group. That's where the discipline kicked in.

In high school, that sense of belonging pulled me deeper into music. I loved it. Once I graduated, I'd even been accepted into the Black Knights Drum Corps, out of Burbank. Our instructor was legendary—intense, precise, relentless. He terrified me. I struggled to meet his exacting pace, the stress turning a tiny patch of my hair gray at the age of 19. But through that crucible I learned syncopation, precision, and performing under pressure.

Meanwhile, I went back to my alma mater to teach drumline. It felt good helping kids understand how to play, how to develop their skills. I kept an eye on *how* they learned, giving analogies that painted vivid pictures. That ability to manage learning styles—seeing what worked for one student versus another—became my first taste of real teaching. I only charged $15 an hour, but even then I knew: I loved teaching, no matter the pay.

From there, I auditioned for the Rochester Patriots Drum & Bugle Corps in New York. The staff drilled me on roll control, hand motion, and how to lock into a section. The next year, I went for the big leagues: Santa Clara Vanguard, one of the top Division I corps in the world. Out of 50 drummers, I made it down to the last 14. And then I got cut.

I was gutted. I returned to the next camp to talk my way back into the corps. But they told me the truth: I needed to make peace with rejection. It was my age-out year. The door had closed.

The MDD Crisis

Eventually, FlashPants—the band I co-founded with my Rich Bro, Graysen—had picked up serious momentum. We were scaling shows, and I was proud of what we'd built. But inside, I hit a strange wall.

I call it *MDD*: Man Deficit Disorder.

I was a successful adult running businesses, teaching, and performing on stages every week. But I had this nagging realization: I didn't actually know how to do many manual things. Woodworking. Metalworking. Welding. Fixing and building with my hands. This was less about becoming a tradesman and more about confidence. I felt like there was a hole in my skill stack, and if I didn't fill it, I wouldn't be prepared for the next stage of life.

So I went looking for answers and found Urban Workshop in Costa Mesa, California, a massive makerspace that offered hands-on classes. I signed up for wood shop, metal shop, and two welding courses: MIG and TIG.

I'll be honest, I wasn't good at it at first. But just learning the basics changed something in me. Suddenly I could walk into a shop and know the difference between a drill press and a band saw. I could weld two pieces of metal together without setting myself on fire. It wasn't mastery, but it was competence. And competence builds confidence.

That short season of tackling my MDD gave me something more valuable than certificates. It reminded me that any deficit can become a stack if you're willing to face it directly. Those elementary skills still pay dividends. Maybe not in dollars, but in self-respect, adaptability, and the quiet confidence that I can figure things out with my hands, not just my head.

Mid-Tier Skills

In 2002, my mom sold our house and moved with my sister and me into a nice apartment in Woodland Hills, California. My sister was coming of age, which meant my dad was no longer obligated to pay child support. I was 20 at that point, scraping by in junior college, and convinced he should keep helping; my own immaturity convinced me that I was still owed. One night my dad called and said, "I love you." I stayed silent. Still, he loved me enough to say the difficult thing I needed to hear: "You need to get a job." That sentence changed my life.

At the time, it stung. Today, I see it as one of the best lessons he ever taught me. He wasn't abandoning me; he was handing me responsibility. And instead of wallowing in self-pity, I heeded his advice and got a job as a host at Islands Restaurant.

I started at the host station, seating guests. Then I moved up to busser, then takeout, then expediter, and finally server. Each step layered new pressure, new expectations, and new abilities. This job wasn't just my first exposure to the crucibles of adulthood, it was an invitation to learn the many ways to successfully work in a team, move efficiently, manage first impressions, and multitask under serious pressure. I could have chosen to think that the job was just about slinging burgers, but it would have done me no good.

By the time I was running a department at Islands, I had already been through a crash course in teamwork, throughput, communication, and service discipline. I had given my pride and self-pity an acid bath.

Several months later, I felt ready to develop my skills further by going into real estate. During the day, I'd knock on hundreds of doors to build my business; at night, I'd manage customers. The hours were brutal, but it was exactly what I needed to turn my natural talents into developed skills. Much like my Dad's advice, it was the bitter medicine I needed. Those experiences developed my grit.

In 2003, I enrolled in the Berklee College of Music Summer Performance Program in Boston. I auditioned into the Tower of Power Ensemble. At first, I was terrible and became outclassed and resented by the rhythm section. But I practiced like a man possessed. Hours every day. By week five, at the final recital, I nailed it. The same players who'd written me off before wanted to be friends.

That summer at Berklee taught me two truths that shaped everything later. One, focused effort compresses time. You can pack years of development into weeks if you're willing to pay the price in intensity. Two, I didn't want to be "a musician." Musicians had no creative control, no ownership, and the economics simply didn't work. Many musicians, whether 10th-best or 100th-best, struggled to get by financially. If I wanted to live as a musician, I had to do it on my own terms. I had to find a way.

Premium Skills: How FlashPants Took Over

When Graysen and I launched FlashPants in 2011, it seemed like it would fail. Years later, when FlashPants exploded in popularity, people thought it was because we were experts in the music industry. They were wrong. We were experts in the *entertainment* business. Let me explain.

The skills I'd developed:

- Drumming (performance, timing, rhythm)
- Real estate sales (grit, rejection management, relationship building)
- Crisis survival (adaptability, resourcefulness, systems creation)

Graysen's skill stack:

- Singing (musical talent, stage performance)
- Touring band experience (his previous group was the most booked act at NACA—the National Association for Campus Activities)
- Long-range vision (pattern recognition, strategic foresight)
- Business systems (process design, efficiency optimization)

Individually, none of this was spectacular. Thousands of people can drum. Thousands can sing. Thousands can sell. But when we combined them, our skills did more than add up; they multiplied.

Consider the Skill Stack of FlashPants:

- **Performance** – Drumming, vocals, bass, guitar, choreography, costuming, lighting, fog machines, large P.A. systems, and scripted stage elements created a full entertainment package.

- **Sales** – Relationship building, rejection handling, and persistence fueled bookings. I cold-called venues, emailed decision-makers, and even walked into bars and clubs with flyers until people said yes.

- **Systems thinking** – Process design and planning turned our band into a business. We built systems that allowed scaling across multiple casts, streamlined logistics for corporate gigs, and created consistency that could be duplicated without us in the room.

Musicians didn't need to be virtuosos, they just had to play the parts, show up on time, and execute. Graysen built custom backing tracks so our shows sounded like the original records people remembered. Purist musicians scoffed, but that's why they stayed broke. Entertainment isn't about you, it's about the audience. If they want to hear a song the way they remember it, you give them that. *It's not about you, it's about the customer.*

The result wasn't just a successful band. It was a reproducible entertainment machine that could scale, dominating high-paying corporate markets, and landing national television appearances in front of millions. That's the difference. Isolated skills make you competent. Stacked skills make you unstoppable.

Chapter 3 Activity: Your Skills Stack Review

It's time to chart your own stack. The goal isn't to admire your list of skills in isolation. Rather, it's to identify the combinations that create exponential leverage. This is where you turn raw materials into structures, and structures into premium stacks.

Your task: Work through the four-step analysis below. Chart your pyramid, spot the combinations, plan your chess upgrade, and map your stacking strategy.

Step 1: Pyramid Mapping

Use your Chapter 2 inventory and sort your skills into the three tiers:

- **Raw Skills (Foundation):**
  - List your baseline human capacities.
  - Include what comes naturally or feels effortless.
  - Don't dismiss the "obvious" ones like communication, problem-solving, resilience.
- **Mid-Tier Skills (Structure):**

- ○ Capture abilities you gained from training or experience.
- ○ Highlight what others consistently compliment you on.
- ○ Note what required deliberate practice to develop.
- **Premium Skills (Current Combinations):**
  - ○ Identify where you already blend multiple skills into something unique.
  - ○ Flag the combinations others consider impressive or hard to replicate.
  - ○ Look for patterns where synergy is already paying off.

Step 2: Identifying Combinations

This is where leverage starts to show up.

- **Current Combinations:**
  - ○ Where are you already using 3+ skills together?
  - ○ Which situations bring out your best work?
  - ○ Where are others relying on you for multi-skill performance?
- **Possible Combinations:**
  - ○ Which mid-tier skills could you fuse for more impact?
  - ○ Where could one new skill dramatically elevate an existing strength?
  - ○ Which pairings align with your interests and goals?
- **Gap Analysis:**
  - ○ What's one skill shy of becoming a powerful blend?
  - ○ Which raw skills should you level up into mid-tier?
  - ○ Where would a strategic addition give you exponential leverage?

Step 3: Chess Piece Upgrade Route

Identify what piece you are on the board, and how to promote yourself.

- **Current Position:**
  - ○ Pawn (limited, replaceable)?
  - ○ Rook (powerful but in narrow lanes)?
  - ○ Knight (unique, but specialized)?

- ○ Bishop (strong diagonally, but limited scope)?
- ○ Queen (versatile, multi-capable, dominant)?
- **Upgrade Strategy:**
  - ○ Which combination would move you to the next level?
  - ○ How could you become harder to replace?
  - ○ What would make you more versatile and valuable in the game?

Step 4: Strategic Stacking Plan

Now turn analysis into action.

- **Priority Combination:**
  - ○ Which skill stack would create the most immediate leverage?
  - ○ Which combination directly addresses your Chapter 1 triage level?
  - ○ Where can you add the most value right now by stacking one more piece onto your current base?
- **Development Plan:**
  - ○ What's the first skill you'll add or refine?
  - ○ How will you practice the *combination*, not just the parts?
  - ○ Where can you test and sharpen this stack in real-world conditions?
- **Timeline:**
  - ○ What could you accomplish in 90 days of focused practice?
  - ○ Where would you be in a year if you stacked with intent?
  - ○ How will you track your progress in stacks, not just individual skills?

This is where theory turns into traction. Stop hoarding skills like spare parts. Build combinations, upgrade your piece, and stack with strategy.

Wrapping It Up

This chapter gave you the Skill Pyramid for categorizing raw, mid-tier, and premium skills and the metaphors and tools to map out your most strategic combinations.

The shift is simple but powerful:

- You stop collecting random skills and start building intentional stacks.

- You stop matching one-to-one skills and start creating unique value through combination.

- You stop hitting ceilings with single abilities and start multiplying leverage through stacking.

That's how you move from being *good at tasks* to being *irreplaceable at the combinations that matter.*

Now that you understand how skills compound, it's time to see this play out under fire. In the next chapter, we'll step into the crucibles, the real-world crises that forced me to stack under pressure and showed me firsthand how adversity can accelerate exponential growth.

CHAPTER 4
THE DOOR-KNOCKER'S EDGE

It does not matter how slowly you go as long as you do not stop.

—Confucius

Priscilla had been grinding at her freelance graphic design business for two years with nothing to show for it. She had talent and an excellent portfolio. But she couldn't lock in steady work.

"I hate the sales part," she confessed to her friend Seth over coffee. "I'm just not aggressive enough. When people say no or brush me off, I take it as they're not interested and move on. Honestly, I've probably only made fifty inquiries in two years."

Seth laughed. "Fifty? I made fifty calls last month for my consulting business."

Priscilla looked shocked. "But isn't that desperate? Like you're harassing people?"

"I used to think the same way," said Seth. "Then my mentor told me something that changed everything: rejection isn't personal feedback, it's math."

She frowned. "What do you mean?"

"Look at it this way. If you're good at what you do, and your service genuinely helps people, then every 'no' isn't a verdict on your worth. It's just someone who isn't your client right now. The no's are clearing the path to the yes's."

"That sounds great," Priscilla said, "but it still feels personal when someone shoots me down."

"That's because you're focused on each rejection instead of seeing the bigger picture. What if you *knew* that one out of every twenty people you reached out to would say yes? Suddenly, each no just moves you closer to that yes."

"So reframing each rejection like a stepping stone to the yes?"

"Exactly. You're not trying to convince everyone. You're finding the people already looking for what you offer."

Priscilla decided to test Seth's approach. She set a simple goal: ten new asks a week, for a month. Each *no* would simply be a tally toward her goal.

Week one: *Eight noes, two no-replies.* Brutal, but she stuck with it. Week two was a little better. Yet by week three, she had finally scored a deal. By week eight, Priscilla's pipeline was full. She didn't radically improve her skills as a designer, nor did she overhaul her portfolio. The only change? She simply reframed rejections as stepping stones to the deals waiting ahead.

*
**

Like Priscilla, you might think you have a "sales problem" or a "networking problem." But often the real block is deeper. It's the perspective, the emotional foundation, the willingness to stay in the game long enough for the odds to work in your favor.

This chapter will show you the template for developing grit, resilience, pattern recognition, and emotional regulation as *trainable skills*. These are the core abilities you can apply anywhere: business, career, relationships, health. And you'll learn how to systematically build them through your own "7,000 doors" challenge.

The Myth of Arrival

Reseda, California. July 2005.

I stood in front of yet another house, clipboard in one hand and a flyer in the other, heart pounding through my chest. I looked like a kid playing dress up: hand-me-down loafers, an old button-down, and a tie older than me. It was 100 degrees. My shirt clung to my back.

And that was the moment it all clicked. Every door I had knocked on, every rejection I had endured, every mile of sidewalk I had trudged had all prepared me for this one. I had just secured my very first real estate listing. It took seven thousand doors to reach my yes.

After bussing tables, scrubbing bathrooms, boxing up takeout orders, and carrying trays at Islands, my business had finally seen some success. I cried on the way back to the office. It was a shining sense of victory, of having finally reached the summit.

The feeling lasted ten minutes.

It hit me: getting that first listing wasn't the end of the struggle. It was the beginning. That moment banished the *Myth of Arrival.*

This myth exists everywhere in culture. We imagine a checkered finish line—some magical moment where the struggle stops, where everything gets easy, where we've finally made it. But in real life, arrival is like the end of a rainbow: an illusion. There is no finish line. There is only *forward.* And if you're fortunate, there is *progress.*

Moonlighting

I didn't have family connections in real estate. My grandmother had been a broker, but she'd retired before I ever started. No mentors, no inherited pipeline, no cushion of money padded my landing into real estate. Just a desire to succeed.

At Islands, I treated bussing like a competition. I tried to move faster than anyone else, clearing and resetting tables before the servers even had to ask. They noticed. The faster their tables turned, the more money they made, and the more they tipped me.

That was my first real lesson in teamwork: when you help others win, they'll take you with them.

When I moved into the food expo role, I struggled. My job was to check every plate against the ticket before it left the kitchen, but my dyslexic brain winced at the details. Mistakes started slipping through; I knew it wasn't my strength. Still, even in failure, I learned something critical: play to your strengths, and build systems or find people to cover your weaknesses.

As a server, I found my groove again. I became one of the top upsellers in the restaurant, turning Well Margaritas into Cadillac Margaritas with just the right phrasing. Not everyone said yes, but I learned to bump my closing percentage, bit by bit. It was a game of inches (an extra dollar here, a few more dollars there) but it added up fast. My sales proved it. And without realizing it, I was learning how to sell, how to read people, and how to share value.

In the mornings, I'd take my lessons learned and hit the streets. I tracked every home I visited, studying well into the night. I wrote every name, even when they'd slammed a door in my face.

There were days when there was no spotlight, no fast cars, no glory. Most days, I was exhausted.

But pushing onward had less to do with emotion—what some call motivation—and more to do with momentum. The grind itself became the fuel. I reframed rejection and mundane door-knocking as stepping stones. Repetitive, unglamorous labor was transformed into a crucible, building me into someone stronger and sharper and grittier.

Looking back, I see what skills I was building. I wasn't trying to launch a real estate career. I was stacking skills that would shape the rest of my life.

What Doorknocking Taught Me

I won't sugar-coat it: door-to-door was a brutal way to build a business. Cold. Seemingly fruitless. Soul-sucking. Every *no* felt personal.

What those 7,000 doors really taught me were four life skills that became the backbone of everything I've done since. And while those first 7,000 doors were just to land my very first deal, I went on to knock on more than 25,000 over the course of my real estate career.

Grit: The Power to Persevere

Grit isn't talent. It isn't luck. It isn't even motivation. Grit is a decision to keep going when motivation runs dry, when your feet ache, when the rain pours down on your parade. Grit is not Instagram-worthy. You don't put grit in a trophy case.

You choose to be gritty, often in silence, when nobody's watching. I'll explain.

- Door 1,000: Still hopeful.
- Door 3,000: Doubting the plan.
- Door 5,000: Wondering if I was wasting my life.
- Door 6,999: Certain it would never work.
- Door 7,000: The one that finally opened.

The lesson isn't that grit pays off quickly. The lesson is that grit gives you the strength to endure long enough for the payoff to come.

As journalist Jacob Riis put it: "when nothing seems to help, I go and look at a stonecutter hammering away at his rock, perhaps a hundred times without as much as a crack showing in it. Yet at the hundred and first blow it will split in two, and I know it was not that last blow that did it, but all that had gone before."

Years later, when I spent months making calls and visiting dive bars to book our first gig for FlashPants, I'd remembered my time in real estate. During

COVID, when I'd taken the leap into financial education, I again thought about those sweltering days in Los Angeles. By then, I knew the program: I could outlast self-doubt.

Resilience: The Art of Bouncing Back

Resilience isn't about taking punishment. It's about recovering quickly and absorbing rejection without losing stride.

Every door became data, not a chance for dejection. Every *not interested* became feedback—about timing, approach, or market fit. It was not a judgment on my worth anymore. That single reframe had a big effect on me.

By door 2,000, I'd stopped taking rejection personally. It was math: a chain of noes led to a *maybe*, and a chain of *maybes* led to a *yes*.

That skill carried over everywhere: On stage with FlashPants when equipment failed mid-show, in classes when students struggled to grasp a concept, in business when deals collapsed. Resilience became my emotional operating system.

Pattern Recognition: The Art of Reading Signals

After thousands of doors, I began noticing patterns others missed: tidy gardens often meant owners who valued long-term investments; cars in the driveway often signalled things about family size, income level, lifestyle priorities; the initial body language with a prospect told me how the entire conversation would go; morning knocks versus evening ones could shift your odds, just as weekdays or weekends could mean a great day versus a wasted one.

Finding patterns about times and neighborhoods translated into pattern recognition at the doorstop. I began to read people and situations instantly, and adjust in real time. *That* skill translated everywhere:

- Feeling the vibe of an audience as FlashPants played
- Spotting when students in financial courses were engaged or drifting
- Distinguishing between serious business leads and tire-kickers

Emotional Regulation: The Art of Remaining Stable

The most valuable thing the doors taught me had nothing to do with property. It was how to keep my inner state independent of external circumstances.

Door-to-door sales gave me the opportunity to:

- Stay optimistic without becoming unrealistic

- Remain professional when prospects weren't

- Push through physical exhaustion

- Project confidence when I felt like an impostor.

- Study my prospects and real estate knowledge, even when I was mentally and physically spent.

That led to developing what I call *emotional flexibility*—the ability to feel disappointment without being crushed by it.

That inner stability became essential everywhere: staying calm amid chaos with FlashPants, projecting confidence as I learned to trade, keeping a fair perspective when business setbacks hit.

How Door-Knocking Skills Apply to Anything

Altogether, these skills formed my emotional operating system. Instead of interpreting a rejection or long workday as signs to quit, I saw them as data points that taught me how to become more resilient. They've become life tools, from door-knocking to dating to drumming in front of millions of viewers.

Dating and Relationships

Having an optimistic (but not unrealistic) approach to dating has taught me that it is similar to sales in many ways. Don't believe me? Like door-knocking, dating is a numbers game: Most interactions won't lead anywhere.

For example, if you're only mutually interested in 5% of people you meet, you'll need to meet 100 to find five matches. The remaining 95 rejections aren't about you—they're part of the process.

The similarities to sales continue. If someone signals that they're interested (such as asking follow-up questions and keeping eye contact), it's different from closed body language or one-word responses.

Another key is finding emotional balance—being authentic without falling into desperation or detachment. Instead of hiding behind squishy language, share your opinions and interests. Be okay with being vulnerable without being needy or aloof.

Persistence is yet another skill that translates to the dating world. Not every relationship will—or should—work out. Continuing to meet new people after breakups, while also making time for yourself, gives you the strength to date from a place of emotional confidence.

Persistence also means holding firm to your values about deal-breakers, while staying open minded to partners outside your "type."

People who struggle in dating almost always lack one of these four skills.

1. They quit too soon (no grit).
2. They take rejection too personally (no resilience).
3. They miss obvious cues (no pattern recognition).
4. They let emotions run the show (no regulation).

Entrepreneurship and Business Development

Every entrepreneur is, in some way, knocking on doors. The product might be different, the market might be bigger, but the skill set is the same.

Grit, for instance, means persisting when prospects aren't buying, revenue isn't rising, or progress isn't visible. I called countless dive bars, shops, and venues to close our first band gig. Graysen and I could have, after months of slow growth, simply lost hope. But we knew that consistency compounds and pushed through.

Being resilient in business means taking noes from investors, customers, and partners without losing hope. Do not personalize rejection. Rather, study your so-called failures: they will teach you about timing, fit, or priorities.

This involves developing your pattern recognition skills. For me, that means reading signals in the markets, customer behavior, and competitors. For example: learning the difference between someone who's truly busy, not merely politely brushing you off. It will save you both time and energy.

Cultivating your pattern recognition skills includes developing your emotional control. This skill has been invaluable, especially during times of uncertainty or difficulty. Making clear decisions under pressure and uncertainty, while keeping your team (or friends or family) confident, is a genuine mark of leadership.

It is easy to spiral into fear or bitterness when the winds of life blow against you. But if you can stay steady amid setbacks, all the while projecting belief in the mission, you become a source not only of hope but joy.

The entrepreneurs who make it in business aren't only the geniuses or most cutthroat machines. Instead, it's those who can stomach the economic, financial, interpersonal storms without losing their ability to push forward.

Chapter 4 Activity: Your Door-Knocker Assessment

Time to find out where your grit, resilience, pattern recognition, and emotional regulation actually stand, and to practice them systematically. This isn't just theory. It's about putting yourself in situations that sharpen your edge.

Your task: Complete the four-step Activity below. Identify your "7,000 doors" challenge, rate your current tolerance, knock on one door this week (literal or metaphorical), and build your daily grit habit.

Step 1: Identify Your Current "7,000 Doors" Issue

Where in your life do you most need to build grit, resilience, pattern recognition, and emotional control?

- **Career/Business**
    - Job search or networking that requires handling rejection.
    - Sales, marketing, or business development where persistence matters.
    - Learning new skills that demand sustained effort.
- **Personal/Relationships**
    - Dating or relationship building that involves risk and rejection.
    - Difficult conversations you've been avoiding.
    - Social situations that push your comfort zone.
- **Health/Lifestyle**
    - Fitness or diet changes that feel slow and unrewarding at first.
    - Breaking habits that take repeated attempts.
    - Forming new habits that feel clunky until momentum builds.
- **Creative/Learning**
    - Skill acquisition that requires fighting through plateaus.
    - Sharing creative work and facing criticism.
    - Learning activities that require persistence with delayed payoff.

Step 2: Rate Your Current Rejection Tolerance (1–10)

- **Grit (Persistence):** How well do you keep going when progress is invisible? Do you quit when things get rough, or do you adapt and keep moving?

- **Resilience (Bounce-Back):** How quickly do you recover after setbacks? Do you see rejection as feedback, or as a verdict on your worth?

- **Pattern Recognition (Reading Signals):** How well do you learn from repetition? Do you spot trends and adjust your approach, or repeat mistakes blindly?

- **Emotional Regulation (Stability):** How effectively do you keep your inner state steady under pressure? Do you remain professional and productive even when stressed?

Step 3: Practice One "Door Knock" This Week

Pick one activity that stretches you into discomfort. Do it.

- **Actual door-knocking:**
  - Business canvassing, volunteering, selling, or networking face-to-face.

- **Metaphorical door-knocking:**
  - Send a connection request, email, or job application you've been avoiding.
  - Start a conversation with someone you'd normally sidestep.
  - Share creative work publicly, despite the risk of criticism.

- **Internal door-knocking:**
  - Have a difficult conversation.
  - Try something brand new outside your comfort zone.
  - Set a boundary you've been afraid to enforce.

Step 4: Build Your Daily Grit Habit

- **Morning Routine:**
  - Set one small goal that forces you to overcome resistance.
  - Do one action that risks rejection or failure.
  - Commit to consistency, not immediate success.

- **Evening Reflection:**
  - Ask: What can I learn from today's setbacks or "no's"?
  - Notice emotional patterns: where you held steady, where you cracked.

- ○ Celebrate persistence, not just results.
- **Weekly Assessment:**
  - ○ Monitor your tolerance for discomfort and rejection.
  - ○ Track progress in staying calm under pressure.
  - ○ Praise yourself for showing up consistently—even if the wins haven't come yet.

This is how you train the Core Four: grit, resilience, pattern recognition, and emotional regulation. One "door knock" at a time.

Wrapping It Up

The door-knocker skills (grit, resilience, pattern recognition, and emotional regulation) are the bedrock. Without them, technical skills are fragile. With them, you can learn anything and survive any transition.

You don't build your future in the spotlight. You build it in the silence of early mornings, in the flurry of effort that doesn't get praise. It is built in the practice sessions—rather than performances—no one sees. It is built one step, one day, one door at a time.

That process of becoming process-oriented is liberating. From then on, you aren't beholden to how much applause, how many likes, or how many deals you close. Instead, you see past the glitz of glory and at the satisfaction of continually improving your skills.

Now that we've covered the foundational skills, it's time to explore the other side: how to use setbacks to accelerate growth.

CHAPTER 5
CRISIS AS CATALYST

Never waste a good crisis.

—Darren, friend and mentor

"You have got to be kidding me," Stephen muttered to himself. He reread the email over and over, thinking that it must have been sent in error. It wasn't. There were no warnings. No red flags. No dramatic crescendo.

Instead, he'd gotten fired through a lousy email. At 45, with a mortgage and two kids in college, Stephen felt like his world had just collapsed.

As they were getting ready for bed, Stephen turned to his wife Sarah in exasperation.

"I don't know what to do," he said.

Sarah had always been the cool and collected one of the two. She gave him a kiss on the forehead.

"Remember when you first started? You had no experience, no contacts, and we'd just had Thomas. Don't you remember how excited you were? You were proactive. You took a temp job at that accounting firm even though it was menial. You used to network with everybody—remember? That three-month contract they offered you turned into a full-time position."

"That was so long ago. I was younger. We had nothing to lose," he said.

"Honey, we were barely scraping by then—with a newborn. We had *a lot* to lose. You made it work."

Stephen sighed. It was true. He could have chosen to give up in the fog of war. Instead, he grew from the experience.

"What about now?" he asked.

"You've got fifteen more years of experience, doesn't that count for something? And you've left such a good impression with the clients you've handled over the years. What if this isn't the end of a career but an opportunity?"

Stephen's eyes lit up. "Like . . . working with multiple companies instead of being tied to just one?"

He rolled out of bed and reached for a pen and pad. It was late, but he was no longer afraid. He was energized.

Three months later, Stephen was using the same financial expertise—now stacked with his new mindset—to start a fractional CFO consultancy. He had learned from Sarah that he could always choose to see crises, like the email, as opportunities for growth.

"The best part of being fired," Stephen told her seven months later, "was remembering what I was really capable of."

*
**

Like Stephen, you may see crises as points of failure. In reality, they serve as crucibles to forge you into a better, stronger, more resilient version of yourself. There's always an upside hidden inside a calamity—if you're ready, willing, and able to do the work.

This chapter will show you how to reframe crises as your greatest accelerator, giving you the tools to mine every setback and carry you into your next breakthrough.

The Blank Page Revelation

In 2009, I spent some time living out of my car.

I had just walked away from the rampant corruption of real estate, idealistic and eager. But idealism doesn't pay rent. My savings had evaporated. My credit cards were maxed out. Job applications seemed to go into the void. No plan B. No rich uncle. Just me and my Chrysler 300M.

At night, I'd park in unlit neighborhoods to try to sleep. I couldn't. The gnawing sense of failure kept me wired. My mind wandered. *Had I made a mistake by leaving the industry? What would my family think of me?* Here I was, dwelling in the dark, sitting in a car that had taken so many prospects to their future homes; in a nasty twist of irony, this car had *become* my home.

In the mornings, I'd splash water on my face in a public restroom before hitting the pavement again, hunting for work or playing small-time gigs. It may sound strange, but I wasn't depressed. I was almost . . . excited. For the first time in my life, everything fake had burned away.

When I was in the industry, I'd enjoyed massive checks, but I did not experience a sense of satisfaction. I'd sold many homes yet could not find pride in it. I had the money, the status, the job title, the reputation.

I'd sometimes lie on the couch, staring blankly, wondering why my success felt so hollow.

So I left. By leaving the industry and everything else behind, I had paradoxically discovered something more valuable than any of those things: the power to choose.

Why Crisis Is Your Best Teacher

Crises don't care about your goals, your ego, or your schedule. They rumble into your life, unbidden and unplanned. What crucial moments like these do is force you to face your authentic self.

A crisis will cause you to let go of the jobs you clung to for too long, the relationships you outgrew, the identities you put on out of convenience, the assumptions you made about what life was *supposed* to be.

Crises leave you exposed, vulnerable, with not so much as a fig leaf to hide behind.

But if you're willing to actually accept crises and learn from them, you find something powerful: yourself—bruised, shaken, but alive.

And so long as you're alive, you can rebuild.

The Roots That Hold

There's an old story that captures this perfectly—the Parable of the Sower, told in multiple Gospels. In Matthew 13, it goes like this:

> *Behold, the sower went forth to sow; and as he sowed, some seeds fell by the way side, and the birds came and devoured them: and others fell upon the rocky places, where they had not much earth: and straightway they sprang up, because they had no deepness of earth: and when the sun was risen, they were scorched; and because they had no root, they withered away. And others fell upon the thorns; and the thorns grew up and choked them: and others fell upon the good ground, and yielded fruit, some a hundredfold, some sixty, some thirty. He that hath ears, let him hear.*

That's how a crisis works. At birth, some of us land in good soil. Some of us land on rocks. But the soil you start with doesn't lock in your outcome. Your job is to grow the deepest roots possible, no matter where you are planted. Shallow roots get scorched the moment life heats up; strong roots endure. And only those that endure eventually grow strong enough to shelter others. This is a concept we visit later on.

Crises test your roots. They don't just expose your conditions; they expose who you are.

Choose Life

In 2019, I developed a fear of flying. It was strange because I'd traveled all over the world—long-haul flights, cross-country tours—and turbulence had never bothered me. But somewhere in my late thirties, on a routine flight to Nashville, it hit me.

Every bump reminded me that the plane could go down, that my life could end there and then. I was suddenly aware of how much unfinished business I had in life—the wife and children I wanted to have, the goals I wanted to accomplish, the lives I wanted to change.

That crisis caused me to see how fragile my existence was, how quickly it could end.

Years later, in 2024, I flew with Graysen on a 15-hour trip to the Philippines. Somewhere over the Pacific, I asked him how he handled fear in the air. He said something simple that landed like a revelation: "I just choose to accept it. Either we die on this flight or we live. But I refuse to sit here in between, trying to control what I can't. I choose it."

That's when it clicked. The opposite of fear isn't control. It's surrender. You can't eliminate turbulence in the air or in your life. You only get to choose whether you fight it or accept it courageously. That choice—to accept the unknown with courage—is freedom.

Stop negotiating with fear, sickness, or doomsday what-ifs. Surrender to the reality that life will carry you exactly as far as it's meant to. Your choice is to live it fully while you can.

As Shakespeare's Julius Caesar said, "A coward dies a thousand times before his death, but the valiant taste of death but once."

The Four Crisis-Developed Skills That Apply Everywhere

I wasn't trying to "develop skills" while living in that car. I was just surviving. But looking back, that season forged four capabilities that became the foundation for everything I built afterward:

Adaptability: The Art of Quick Adjustment

Living in my car forced me to function when everything shifted, using whatever was available, staying productive in uncomfortable conditions, making the best of unstable environments.

That ability became critical later—when FlashPants faced canceled venues or failed equipment, and when COVID had erased the entire entertainment industry overnight.

Resourcefulness: The Art of Maximum Leverage

Resourcefulness isn't about getting more; it's about squeezing every ounce of value from what you have.

In the car, I learned to:

- Use public gyms for showers and libraries for the internet
- Leverage free resources: networking at events with food and nabbing samples at grocery stores
- Turn casual conversations into opportunities
- Stretch one dollar until it worked like five

Later, that sense showed up everywhere: starting FlashPants without capital, creating costumes from scraps, generating marketing buzz on a shoestring budget, and launching my consulting business by leveraging existing relationships and knowledge instead of chasing funding.

Opportunity Recognition: The Art of Seeing Potential

Opportunity recognition isn't blind optimism—it's spotting potential where others only see problems.

My car saga taught me to:

- Spot hidden upside in bad circumstances

- Reframe setbacks as detours instead of dead ends
- Seek opportunities in places others ignored
- Distinguish between temporary and lasting conditions

That perspective shift altered the rest of my life. When a friend mentioned a drummer was needed, I sought to make the most of the opportunity. To my surprise, in my initial conversation, I saw Graysen's lofty vision for *what the band could be*. I saw his drive and tenacity, his work ethic and like-mindedness. In that moment FlashPants was born.

Had we stuck to the "reality" of being yet another cover band, we would have never had the gumption to land our first gig. Had we been unable to reframe the setbacks of bad nights or unexpected equipment failures onstage, we'd never been able to get to over 200 shows annually. Put simply, our grit and resourcefulness paved the way to our success.

Crises come for us all. They eat away your ego and self-concept. It is up to you, however, to use those moments to sharpen your skills and come back stronger.

Mental Resilience: The Art of Inner Stability

Mental resilience isn't about brute force. It's about staying calm, focused, and consistent when the world is ablaze. The car life taught me to focus on the next step instead of the overwhelming big picture, and to trust that temporary conditions wouldn't become my permanent identity

Mental stability became essential in navigating the turbulence of business. More than once, a gig fell through with guys already on the payroll. We'd have to make the most of it. In the investing world, when teaching high-level concepts that didn't land, I'd pivot in real time to ensure everyone understood fully.

It is a fact of life that crises arrive without invitation. But they come bearing gifts, if you're keen enough to spot them.

The Reframe That Changes Everything

Most people waste their crises because they're desperate to rewind, to get "back to normal." They ask: "How can I get out of this quickly?" or "Why me?"

Before you fall into this trap, remember that our greatest development often comes from adversity. We have the power to reframe our situations, thereby maximizing our chances of coming out of them stronger, better, happier.

The shift is to ask:

- "What skill is this situation forcing me to build?"
- "What assumptions is this revealing that need to be improved upon?"
- "How might this be guiding me somewhere better?"

The crisis is not the problem. Wasting the crisis is the problem.

After I got back from the Philippines, I signed up for flying lessons at the local airport. I wanted to desensitize myself and understand what's actually happening in the air—how lift works, how the plane holds itself up, what the mechanics are instead of just trusting a metal tube on faith.

My instructor handed me the controls and let me fly the Cessna for a while. It felt like piloting a 1970s VW Bug in the sky—loud, shaky, and honest. And it was an especially bumpy day, according to him.

It didn't matter. I kept the plane level and proved to myself I could handle it.

That experience, combined with the increased flying since, has had a wonderful effect on me: I don't fear flying anymore.

Chapter 5 Activity: Your Crisis Catalyst Inventory

It's time to mine your crises for the skills they gave you and extract maximum value from the challenges you're facing right now.

Your task: Complete the four step analysis below. Identify your past crucibles, name the transferable skills, reframe current struggles, and design a strategy to maximize every ounce of value from what you're going through.

Step 1: Past Crisis Inventory

List 3–5 major challenges from the past decade:

- Loss of employment or career stagnation
- Relationship breakup or family crisis
- Physical setback or health scare
- Financial loss or pressure

- Major life disruption or loss

For each, ask:

- What skill did this crisis force me to build?

- How did I adapt to survive or thrive?

- What resourcefulness did I discover?

- What opportunities were hidden that I couldn't see at the time?

Step 2: Identification of Skills Transfer

- **Soft skills:** What did you learn about adapting to new conditions? How did you stay effective despite disruption?

- **Resourcefulness:** What creative solutions did you come up with? How did you stretch what you had?

- **Opportunity recognition:** What signals did you learn to look for? What doors opened only because of that crisis?

- **Mental toughness:** How did you maintain stability inside while chaos raged outside? What did you learn about separating temporary conditions from permanent identity?

Step 3: The Blank Page Test

List 3 areas of uncertainty in your life right now:

- Career or business challenges needing transformation

- Relationship dynamics requiring work

- Health or lifestyle areas to improve

- Financial constraints needing new solutions

- Creative or personal projects that feel stuck

For each, ask:

- What if this obstacle is building skills I'll need later?

- What assumptions about "how life should work" need to be broken?

- What hidden opportunity might be inside this problem?

Step 4: Resource Maximization Strategy

- **Daily Crisis Reframing:** When you hit resistance, ask: *"What skill is this* *building?"* Spot one small win inside every setback. Separate inner state from external events.

- **Weekly Opportunity Scan:** Review challenges for hidden potential. Pick one creative solution to test each week. Track the skills being forged through repetition.

- **Monthly Progress Review:** Write down what strengths you've gained from your current struggles. Note how skills from past crises are helping now. Reward skill development, not just visible wins.

Wrapping It Up

A crisis is not your enemy. Crises are the most intense training program you'll ever experience—if you know how to use them.

That week I spent living in my car wasn't the worst week of my life. You may not believe me. But it stripped away everything unnecessary and forced me to develop the core skills that later powered FlashPants, that made my pivot into financial education possible, and that fueled every reinvention that followed.

That crisis was one of the best seasons of my life.

To tell you the truth, if "normal" was working, you wouldn't be in a crisis. Crises show up because something old is broken. Instead of running from your blank page moments, dig in. Mine them. Treat them as laboratories for developing the skills you don't yet know you'll need.

The abilities you build in crises aren't just survival tactics. They're the foundation on which you'll construct everything that comes next.

Now that you've seen how crises build foundational skills, the next step is learning how to stack them strategically. This is where momentum explodes and where skills from one domain create exponential breakthroughs in completely different ones.

CHAPTER 6
THE RICH BRO BLUEPRINT

Perfection is achieved not when there is nothing more to add, but when there is nothing left to take away.

—Antoine de Saint-Exupéry

Rebekah had been grinding as a freelance marketing consultant for three years. Skilled. Diligent. Clients loved her. And yet, every quarter ended the same: revenue stuck at $8K a month.

"I don't get it," she vented to her friend Isaac over lunch. "I'm working 60-hour weeks, my clients adore me, and I still can't break through. When I tried to raise my rates or take on bigger projects, I hit a ceiling. I can't seem to grow any further."

Isaac leaned back. "You're making the classic mistake. You're running your business like a one-woman band. You're trying to do *everything* yourself. What you need isn't more hours. It's leverage."

Rebekah frowned. "Leverage how?"

"My business partner taught me the most important shift I ever made," Isaac said. "Stop trying to be the smartest person in every room. Start focusing on being the best orchestrator. You don't have to do every task yourself. You just have to control the outcome. That's how you scale."

"But where do I even find someone like that? And why would they want to work with me?"

"Start with the people you already know," Isaac replied. "Think about the freelancers you've collaborated with who have complementary skills. Who impressed you? Who has the strengths you don't?"

Rebekah paused. "There's this brand strategist, Sarah. Brilliant at vision and positioning. I'm more of an execution person. Every time we worked together, she blew me away."

"Perfect," Isaac said. "Don't pitch a permanent partnership. Start with one project. Approach her about solving a client problem together. If it works, you'll both see the potential."

Three months later, Rebekah and Sarah had built a system. Sarah handled strategy and vision. Rebekah ran implementation and operations. Their first joint client was so successful that word spread, and new clients began demanding the same integrated service.

*
**

Like Rebekah, you may be stuck in independent thinking. This means you might be trading time for money, maxing out your capacity, and confusing effort with scale. The unlock is interdependent thinking. This chapter will show you how to find, court, and build partnerships that expand your capacity and transform you from solo operator to systems orchestrator.

Broadnet, Dial-Up and a Lunch-Break Pivot

Before FlashPants, my days were spent in a fluorescent box at a company called Broadnet Solutions, cold-calling remote pockets of California where, yes, people were still on dial-up in 2011. We sold "high-speed" satellite internet that needed line of sight to a mountain relay. If the tech didn't show (there was basically one guy) or the weather killed the signal, the customer's fury came straight to me.

Two hundred calls a day taught me to pitch quickly before the hang-up, to listen for real pain, and to absorb blowback from problems I didn't cause but still had to solve. It was gritty, unglamorous rep-building.

Then, one day over a lunch break, my phone buzzed. It was Graysen. We'd workshopped an '80s dance concept, maybe even a Star Wars/Star Trek twist, but nothing set in stone. I remember pacing the hallway, headset off, getting more excited with each idea bubbling up. At that moment, I realized I didn't want to sell janky internet forever. I wanted to build something people couldn't ignore. I wanted to take the joy of beating a new path for myself.

That call became the beginning and the end: broadnet in the rearview, FlashPants on the horizon.

Mini-Lesson: What Selling Bad Internet Taught Me About Stacking

- **Compress the pitch.** Lead with the one sentence that matters most before the hang-up window closes.
- **Listen for the *real* problem.** Tech issues, missed appointments, unmet expectations: name it, own it, solve it.

- **De-escalate fast.** Anger often isn't about you; it's about broken systems. Stay steady and move the ball.

- **Own outcomes without control.** You can't control the weather or the tech's calendar: only the next best step.

- **Log patterns.** If the same issue repeats, it's not a one-off. It's a process fix or positioning problem.

- **Practice honest fit.** Sometimes the best "sale" is telling someone they're not a fit. Credibility compounds.

- **Convert reps into assets.** Those phone skills later powered booking, crowd work, and corporate sales.

Takeaway: Even "throwaway" jobs stack real advantages (communication, emotional regulation, pattern recognition) that become rocket fuel once you plug into the *right* vehicle and the *right* partner.

Background Acting & the Ownership Lesson

Before Real Estate, before Broadnet, before FlashPants, I chased the Hollywood dream. I dove into background acting and enjoyed some success. Central Casting was my pipeline. I landed gigs as a waiter on *Miss Match* with Alicia Silverstone, a photo double for David Caruso on *CSI: Miami*, even a drummer in *Dodgeball* (you can spot me around the 6-minute mark with my back to the camera). On *American Dreams*, I even danced with Brittany Snow. It's possible that I even hold the world record for the most number of background appearances in one minute on a feature film.

It wasn't glamorous. The pay was low, the craft services were the highlight, and the A-list actors often looked down on us. The bigger realization was that I didn't like it: I wasn't wired to memorize lines or wait for casting directors to hand me permission. If I was going to be in entertainment, it had to be *on my own terms*: my show, my script, my rules. I thought of Robert Frost's "The Road Not Taken":

I shall be telling this with a sigh

Somewhere ages and ages hence:

Two roads diverged in a wood, and I—

I took the one less traveled by,

And that has made all the difference.

The words floated in my head on especially bad days—days when I dreamed about having some autonomy. The dreams felt unreachable then. But they set the stage for what made FlashPants so magnetic an idea when it finally arrived. Flashpants was a chance at taking the road less traveled.

The Partnership That Changed Everything

In 2011, I was broke, drifting, and had been out of real estate for a few years. That's when a mutual friend introduced me to Graysen. He needed a drummer for a new band he was putting together.

But this wasn't going to be just another bar band grinding for beer money. Graysen had a bigger vision: a scalable entertainment company in the spirit of Blue Man Group. A band that wasn't just about gigs, but about building a brand that could outgrow its founders.

I was flat broke, but I was all in.

And what would eventually become FlashPants started as two guys building something larger than themselves.

Graysen became my Rich Bro, not because he had deep pockets, but because he had a deep understanding of his mission. He was rich in experience, foresight, and the ability to spot bottlenecks before they choked growth. From him, I learned two forces that drive reinvention more than anything else: interdependence and identity transfer.

The FlashPants Origin Story

Those early days were chaos wrapped in spandex.

We started with Party City costumes that looked like Halloween clearance leftovers. One of my first brilliant name suggestions? *Dance Dance the Dance Band.* (Yes, seriously.)

Graysen even floated a concept called *Star Star*, which involved stormtroopers and redshirt Star Trek characters. Fun idea…until you realize those costumes would've been sweaty death traps under stage lights.

Through trial and error, we stumbled onto the look that stuck: red dolphin shorts, red-and-white tank tops, and fake mustaches. Quirky. Loud. Unmistakable. And yes, unashamedly sexy.

Our first gig was at The Cobra Club, a gay Hispanic bar in North Hollywood that paid $400 for Wednesday nights. The audience loved us—and we loved them—but they weren't our long-term market.

The real proving ground came at The Canyon Inn in Yorba Linda, CA. Every Thursday night for a year and a half, we sold out the place. That's where we sharpened the act, tested bits, learned timing, and figured out how to make *any* demographic laugh, dance, and cry.

By 2014, we knew what it would take to scale: clean up the raunch, tighten the show, and package it for corporate clients who were ready to spend real money.

What began as chaos evolved into a sophisticated entertainment machine, a band, a brand, and eventually, a business that could run on systems.

The Day I Took Responsibility

At first, I focused on drumming and brainstorming. Graysen handled everything else: bookings, promotions, logistics, costumes, frontman duties. The entire band was on his back, and I could see it was wearing him down.

One day it hit me: *This isn't just Graysen's band; this is my band, too.* I offered to take some administrative duties.

Then I dove headfirst into operations, marketing, and backend systems. While most of the guys just wanted to play music, Graysen and I were building something bigger. We knew it would take work.

Together, we turned FlashPants into a real business; planned schedules and organized casts; systematized marketing campaigns; automated bookings and contract generation; built review engines that fueled growth; and expanded into multiple casts performing across the state.

Staking a claim to ownership without waiting to be invited changed not only the band, but me. It became an invitation to take responsibility.

My Rich Bro: Rich in Wisdom, Not Money

Graysen wasn't wealthy when I met him. Neither of us were. But he was rich where it mattered:

- He thought 5–10 years ahead, not 5–10 days.

- He saw systems where others saw chaos.

- He fixed bottlenecks before they became crises.

- He believed success should be replicated, not reinvented from scratch.

By working alongside him, part osmosis, part trial by fire, I began rewiring my own operating system.

What Graysen taught me:

- Skill stacking beats single-lane mastery.

- Clone what works, don't rebuild from scratch.

- Systems thinking turns dreams into durable realities.

- Bottlenecks aren't tactical annoyances. Really, they are strategic killers.

Graysen helped shape FlashPants, to be sure, but he also influenced me.

I still live by some of the maxims that came out of those years. Two, in particular, were from *The Wrecking Crew*, a documentary about LA musicians who played on thousands of records—often without credit.

One was: "The only time it's okay to say no to a gig is when you're too busy to say yes." That prodded us to take gigs even when we were tired or when they didn't seem promising. Another reminded us that show business was not only about shows but about business: "those who work, work."

The most important one did not come from the documentary but from Graysen. Whenever we'd begin stargazing or considering gigs that truly were wrongheaded, he'd say, "the income always affects the outcome." It was always the right call, the perfect words to bring us back to reality.

These simple adages didn't just sound good as bumper stickers. They became the lifeblood of our young business, guiding us through the toughest stages (literally) of a startup.

Reinvention Skill Spotlight: Manage the Job, Not the Tasks

One of the most powerful lessons Graysen drilled into me was deceptively simple: "You don't have to do everything yourself. You only need to manage the position."

Leadership isn't about burning yourself out doing every task. It's about owning the *outcome*, whether you create it, delegate it, or build a system that produces it on autopilot.

That single shift unlocked exponential growth:

- I built systems instead of putting out fires.

- I focused on high-leverage moves instead of busywork.

- I scaled without losing my sanity.

Highlight the function, not the details. That principle has stacked into every business, teaching role, and leadership position I've ever held since.

Turbo Journaling: A Powerful Rich Bro Tool for Clarity

Graysen introduced me to a deceptively simple but brutally effective tool: **Turbo Journaling.**

Whenever I was stuck, spinning out, or trapped in my own head, he'd say: "Go walk. Talk. Record. Then listen to yourself."

When you play it back, you hear the unfiltered and unvarnished truth—you hear exactly where you're stuck, the loops you keep repeating, and the truth about what needs to change.

The process is simple:

1. Walk and talk – movement clears the mind.

2. Record a voice memo – stream-of-consciousness, no filter.

3. Play it back immediately – confront your raw honesty.

4. Identify the patterns – note the ideas or complaints you repeat.

I talk to myself out loud every single day—not because I'm losing it or because I'm lonely, but because it genuinely works. It helps me process, plan, think, lead, and make decisions faster than anything else I've ever tried. Over time, it's become one of the most reliable tools in my entire reinvention stack. I'll be in the car, in the shower, or walking down the street just talking. And yeah, sometimes people look at me sideways, or I'll crack myself up with something I say out loud. I don't care. It's productive, it's real, and honestly, it's powerful.

The funny thing is that everybody accepts journaling as healthy. Therapists recommend it, coaches swear by it, authors build entire systems around it. But when you think about it, journaling is really just writing to yourself. So if writing to yourself is good, talking to yourself can be even better—especially for someone like me who thinks way faster than I can write. Instead of waiting for words to slowly drip onto a page, I speak them. I listen, respond, challenge myself, pivot mid-sentence. I take the storm inside my head and bring it out into the world where I can actually work with it.

Most people don't realize how much their inner dialogue shapes their outcomes. Your thoughts aren't passive; they're generative.

Turbo Journaling became my go-to clarity weapon. No technique clears mental fog faster. It has guided every major decision I've made since. If you've never tried it, give yourself sixty seconds. You'll be surprised by what comes out when you finally let it.

Chapter 6 Activity: Your Rich Bro Blueprint Review

It's time to identify the "Rich Bros" in your world, confront your independence blind spots, and practice managing outcomes instead of drowning in tasks.

Your assignment: Work through the four-step blueprint below.

Step 1: Discover Your Rich Bro

Ask yourself:

- Who thinks 5–10 years ahead while you're stuck planning 5–10 days?

- Who sees systems where you see chaos?

- Who has strengths that fill your blind spots?

- Who eliminates friction before it becomes a problem?

Needed Rich Bro Profile:

- Where do you need someone with long-range vision?

- What blind spots keep slowing your growth?

- What kind of strategic partner would unlock scale?

- Where are you trying to do everything solo when teamwork would be smarter?

Step 2: Balance Independence vs. Interdependence

Rate yourself (1–10):

Current Operating Mode

- How often do you insist on doing it all yourself?
- Are you managing tasks or managing jobs?
- Are you creating systems, or just firefighting?

Partnership Readiness

- How well do you share ownership without losing control?
- Can you focus on outcomes instead of micromanaging process?
- Do you actively look for chances to blend strengths with others?

Analysis:

- Where are you too independent for your own good?
- Where could interdependence create exponential outcomes?
- What alliance could you pursue this month?

Step 3: "Manage the Position" Practice

Pick one area where you're currently drowning in tasks.

Current Task Audit:

- What are you doing right now that could be systematized?
- Where are you supervising activities instead of managing outcomes?
- What bottlenecks exist because everything flows through you?

Position Upgrade:

- What's the outcome you could manage instead of executing?
- How could you make that outcome happen without doing the work yourself?
- What process or system could you build to solve this once and for all?

This Week's Experiment:

- Choose one task you currently own.
- Define the desired outcome clearly.
- Practice managing the position instead of doing the work.

Step 4: Turbo Journaling Startup

Commit to the **Turbo Journaling** method for one week:

Daily Practice:

- Take a 10–15 minute walk and talk through a current challenge.
- Record your stream of consciousness on your phone.
- Listen back immediately: no editing, no filters.
- Note recurring patterns, blind spots, and insights.

Weekly Review:

- What themes kept repeating in your recordings?
- Where did you catch yourself in self-deception?
- What clarity emerged that silent reflection never gave you?

Prompts to explore in your sessions:

- Where am I micromanaging tasks instead of managing positions?
- What alliance could accelerate my current goals?
- Where am I stuck in tactics when I should be thinking strategically?
- What system could I design to eliminate daily friction?

Wrapping It Up

You don't have to reinvent yourself alone. In fact, you *shouldn't*. The fastest growth often comes through proximity, when you align with someone whose vision outpaces yours until it becomes your own.

Graysen is an upstanding guy who won't just hand you strategies. He helped me with an identity and mindset upgrade.

Through synergy, I built skills faster than I ever could alone. Through identity transfer, I stopped being "just the drummer" and became a big-picture thinker, strategist, and leader.

And here's the kicker: being someone's Rich Bro is just as powerful as having one.

When you master partnership skills, you don't just find the right people; you *become* the person others seek out. You become the partner who multiplies strength, clears bottlenecks, and scales vision.

Find your Rich Bro or Bro-ette. Become someone else's Rich Bro. Learn to share a vision. Build interdependent power greater than anything you could achieve alone.

Because real reinvention isn't always about doing more. Sometimes it's about *becoming something more...* through the multiplied strength of strategic partnership.

And once you've got the right partnerships in place, there's a new challenge: systems. Partnerships only scale if the backbone holding them up is strong. That's where we're headed next, into the operational frameworks that turn collaboration into a machine.

CHAPTER 7
FROM CHAOS TO MACHINE

The best way to predict the future is to create it.

—Peter Drucker

Adam was the new sourcing manager for a small textile manufacturer. Though he'd only been on the job for a few months, he had a string of red X's and missed deadlines looming on his calendar. It ate away at him.

The division Adam had taken over was not lazy, but it was disorganized. Some days, meetings would extend endlessly, without a clear objective or outcome. One meeting went over by 30 minutes, without a clear outcome in sight. Projects went unfinished.

One day, an old friend from the manufacturing division, Mark, came to visit Adam at his office.

Adam shared his struggles.

"Every project feels like starting from scratch," Adam said. "Everyone has their own filing system, their own way of talking to clients. If someone takes a vacation, their work basically dies on the vine."

Mark listened patiently. "Do you have a people problem or a systems problem?" he asked.

Adam thought about the last meeting---the silence when he asked who owned the next step. No one had answered, but no one had looked confused either.

"It's a systems problem," he admitted.

"Perfect," said Mark. "The first step to change is admitting that you have a problem. Now we come to action. What's the smallest system that you could implement right now to improve your meeting outcomes?"

"I guess our meetings could have just one goal," Adam said.

"Wonderful, just one goal. And what next. . .?"

For two hours they talked about the fuzzy deadlines, unclear expectations, and feel-it-out "systems" bogging the division down.

The changes were immediate: Adam's team members were pleasantly surprised to find that meetings were shorter. They were focused. They were even *exciting*. But Adam didn't stop there. Over the next month, he standardized project folders, client communication templates, and hand-off checklists.

After a few months, Adam's team was humming along nicely. His division started hitting deadlines, exceeding expectations. And Management noticed.

*
**

Like Adam, you may think of disorder as a sign of laziness, when in reality, it's strangling your growth. This chapter will show you how to build systems that *scale your genius without suffocating it*, giving you the templates to transform any chaotic process into a machine that runs clean, fast, and free.

Frappuccino Hell

Long before I was scaling FlashPants, I was behind a Starbucks counter in Granada Hills, California. I worked there for two years, and while it wasn't glamorous, it was my first real lesson in systems under pressure.

Our store sat right next to my old high school, which meant that every weekday at 2:30 p.m., the floodgates opened. Hundreds of teenagers swarmed in at once, demanding one thing: frappuccinos. We called it *Frappuccino Hell*. Huge frozen cups of whipped sugar and caffeine, exactly what every 15-year-old needs, right? (Still not sure where their parents were, but that's another story.)

To survive the rush, we had to change the way we worked. Instead of making drinks one at a time, we prepped pitchers in bulk, batched orders, and created a whole new workflow just to keep up. Some kids even ordered what they called a "suicide frappuccino": one pump of every syrup we had, all blended together. Disgusting, but they loved it.

Outside the chaos, I learned the art of anticipation. I knew my regulars' drinks so well I'd start making them as soon as I saw their cars pulling into the lot. I learned to remember names, pick up conversations where we'd left off, and make each transaction feel personal. Tips weren't just about speed, they were about connection.

Looking back, Starbucks was an early crucible. It taught me to optimize workflow when the pressure was highest, to create repeatable systems when chaos threatened to overwhelm, and to build relationships in the middle of the grind.

Those skills (anticipation, pattern recognition, speed, and connection) became the seeds of everything I would later scale in bands, business, and teaching.

Stacking Proactivity

Of course, anticipation isn't just about customer service. It can be life or death.

A few years ago, driving home from LA on Christmas, I hit rain-soaked pavement on the 101 near Cahuenga. I wasn't speeding. But suddenly my car lost traction, spun 360 degrees, and slammed into the center divider. Airbags exploded, my wrists took the hit, and I came to a stop facing oncoming traffic.

For a split second, everything went silent. Then instinct said *run*. I bolted into the ditch as my car, still in drive, crept forward toward oncoming traffic. By sheer grace, it veered into an embankment before anyone was hit.

Later, replaying it in my mind, I remembered what I'd been ignoring: my right rear tire was fairly bald. I knew it. I kept driving on it anyway. Maybe the tread wasn't the only factor, but in my gut I believe it mattered. And if it did, the entire accident came down to one thing: my failure to act on what I already knew.

That's the real lesson: stack proactivity.

Systems aren't just built to react, they're built to *prevent*. A bald tire, an outdated process, an unchecked assumption. Small cracks become full-scale chaos if you don't address them in time.

Proactivity is a stackable skill. Build it into everything:

- Replace the tire before the spinout.
- Fix the broken process before it costs a client.
- Address the relationship tension before it blows up.
- Maintain the machine so it doesn't collapse under load.

The best systems are the ones that keep you from hitting the wall.

The White Collar Crew

In late 2007, I wandered into a Super Crown bookstore (back when those still existed) and picked up Tim Ferriss's *The 4-Hour Workweek*. It flipped the script on my understanding of business. I could leverage my skills, my effort, and build systems instead of trading time for money. If other people could systematize their lives and businesses, why couldn't I?

Within weeks I launched my own experiment: The White Collar Crew, a full-service, anything-virtual company. Business cards, Photoshop, web design, translations, you name it. I sold the work locally, then outsourced most of it overseas through freelancer platforms in India.

On paper, it was genius: I'd be the middleman, pocketing the spread while other people did the heavy lifting. In practice, it was chaos.

- Clients wanted midnight edits, but my overseas team was asleep.

- One web developer disappeared mid-project, taking my money and leaving me to refund a client I'd already promised a finished site.

- I loved the project management side, but hated having no control over the final delivery.

The business folded fast. But the lessons stuck:

- **Systems thinking:** Coordinating multiple projects across time zones.

- **Delegation awareness:** Learning what *can* be outsourced, and what should never leave your hands.

- **Risk management:** Always build fail-safes before promising outcomes.

- **Control variables:** True scale means owning the levers that matter most.

I even dreamed up a spinoff called The Blue Collar Crew, a moving-labor business, but didn't yet have the leadership skills to manage a team of guys.

Mini-Lesson: Not every system you build will last. But every system you test teaches you something. The White Collar Crew was my first outsourcing experiment. It failed as a business, but it stacked the project management, delegation, and accountability skills I'd later use to scale bands, consulting, and classrooms.

The Scaling Challenge

By 2014, FlashPants had grown from the chaotic startup Graysen and I cobbled together into a California entertainment staple. But this success created a new kind of pain.

I leaned on my old real estate cold-calling playbook to hustle gigs. Grit paid off, we landed our first residency, steady income, and a live laboratory to refine the act. But within months, growth outpaced our setup.

TV spots, weddings, corporate events, gigs poured in. And with them came chaos: canceled shows, double-bookings, equipment breakdowns. We were drowning in our own momentum.

We'd outgrown the bars, but the corporate world, tech firms, casinos, big brands, expected polish. They didn't want raunchy antics that could spark HR complaints. They wanted reliability. In 2014, we pivoted hard: trimmed the edgiest bits, kept the humor, made it HR-friendly without losing our soul. That shift turned us from bar-band novelty into a corporate entertainment product.

The payoff was real. In 2015 we hit the South Point Casino showroom in Vegas, playing to hundreds of suits. We nailed it, but only because we'd built a backend machine strong enough to carry the weight.

Machine Construction: The Four Core Systems

Scaling almost broke us: booking errors, cash flow scares, ego clashes. The turning point was building systems that could run without constant firefighting. Four pillars emerged: brand, leadership, process, and scale.

1. Brand Building: Getting It to Stick

A brand isn't what you *say* about yourself. It's what people *feel* the second they see you.

Our brand locked in around three elements:

- **Visual identity:** red shorts, tank tops, mustaches, visible from 100 yards.

- **Energy signature:** ridiculous, shameless, self-depricating, inclusive, high-octane fun.

- **Consistent experience:** same format, same audience participation, same payoff every time.

The Shake Weight competition, Lady & The Tramp Skit, Gummy Worm contest and Gangnam Style Schtick, drove this home: brand isn't designed in a boardroom, it's discovered by trial and error. Some experiments bombed. Others became staples. We doubled down on what stuck. You can see one such skit here:

That clarity gave us leverage:

- We could train new members quickly in "The FlashPants Way."
- We could guarantee clients the same result, every time.
- We could command premium booking fees because people knew exactly what they were buying.

2. Team Leadership: Leading from Behind

I learned fast: leading didn't mean being the star. It meant making the system of stars work.

Graysen fronted the band; I played drums. His knack for show business meant that he handled those aspects extremely well. I took over the business engine behind those systems. Together, we grew leadership from personality-based to process-based.

Our principles:

- **Own without ego:** chase results, not credit.
- **Systems over personalities:** keep processes bigger than any individual.
- **Defined roles, shared ownership:** clear accountability, collective pride.
- **Lead by serving:** clear obstacles so performers could shine.

Example:

- Our guitarist Micah handled staffing and scheduling for multiple casts.
- Our bassist Josh edited training videos so new members could learn from home.
- We built a playbook that captured not just the setlist but the *energy, humor, and crowd work* that defined the brand.

Of course, more people meant more egos. Musicians clashed. Graysen, our "papa bear", kept the peace with firmness and kindness. When he burned out, I learned to step into that role, guiding through structure instead of dominance.

3. Process Creation: Systems That Run Without You

The biggest breakthrough came when I stopped trying to do everything myself and started building systems that ran without me.

Key processes we locked in:

- **Booking pipeline:** CRM to track leads, automated reminders, contract generators.
- **Rehearsals:** Standardized setlists, choreography videos, gear checklists.
- **Performance standards:** Costume requirements, show flow, scripted audience interactions.
- **Payments:** Automated billing, expense tracking, and scheduled payouts.

I built spreadsheets, templates, and workflows for everything: scheduling, follow-ups, equipment, contracts. Not to stifle creativity, but to create a structure where creativity thrived without collapsing under chaos.

4. Scale Management: Cloning Success

The real test came when we scaled beyond the first lineup. We cloned the FlashPants show—with different castmembers—into second, third, even fourth groups across California, all wearing the same shorts, mustaches, and attitude. Learning what scaled and what didn't taught us how to grow a business efficiently. Those lessons were crucial when we expanded into Arizona.

Scaling required:

- **Replicable training:** Video-based onboarding + practice sessions.
- **Quality control:** Regular check-ins to keep every cast on-brand.
- **Resource allocation:** Costumes, props, and gear shared efficiently.
- **Performance monitoring:** Tracking which casts excelled and which needed support.

By 2016, we were pulling off 200+ shows a year. Not because we were better musicians, but because our machine was designed to outperform any single-lineup band still reinventing the wheel every gig.

The Pizza Kitchen That Taught Me Systems

In 2013, I worked as a delivery driver for Fresh Brothers Pizza at the Santa Monica location. It wasn't just a job, it was a front row seat to entrepreneurship. I was lucky enough to work side by side with the founders themselves, the Goldberg family: Scott, Adam, Mike, and even their dad. Scott and I would swap stories in the kitchen while slinging pies, and I learned as much from those conversations as I did from any business book.

One night, Scott handed me a delivery ticket that made my jaw drop: Adam Sandler's house in the Pacific Palisades. I pulled up in my beat-up Chrysler 300M at the exact same time Sandler rolled in with his black Escalade. We walked in together like it was staged. In the kitchen, he looked at me and said, "Thanks for bringing me dinner!" I managed to get out, "I appreciate your work." Then his daughters ran in yelling, "Daddy, Daddy, we're watching Finding Nemo 3!" and he, in full Sandler voice, replied, "Of course you are, 'cause it's the best one!" It felt like I'd stumbled onto a movie set, only it was real life, and I was the pizza guy.

Not every moment was Hollywood magic. Once, Adam Goldberg saw my car with a kick drum tossed in the backseat and said, "It looks like you're living in your car." He wasn't entirely wrong. My jeans were shredded, and he pulled me aside: "You can't wear those here, we've got high-end clientele." He was right, and I laughed it off, but inside I knew he was teaching me something about presentation and professionalism.

Scott even came to an early FlashPants show once in Santa Monica, standing in the crowd watching me in a completely different world than the pizza kitchen. Not long after I left Fresh Brothers, the Goldbergs sold to private equity and made a killing. I couldn't have been happier for them. By the time you're reading this, there's a good chance Fresh Brothers is a national pizza chain.

I believe it's possible that Adam Sandler's Palisades house burned down in the recent fires, but that house will live on in my mind forever.

That experience reminded me: systems don't just scale bands, they scale pizza shops, classrooms, consulting firms, and entire industries.

The Disneyland Rule: Pay Yourself First

In 2016, I was in a relationship that revolved around Disneyland. We'd head to Downtown Disney or into the park itself. Every trip meant blowing a few hundred dollars on food and tickets and trinkets. The problem was: money was still tight that year. I couldn't afford to part with hundreds of dollars so often. Driving to the "Happiest Place on Earth" made my gut go into knots.

Around that time, I had just started dabbling in precious metals, small buys of gold and silver. It gave me an idea: if I was going to spend $200 at Disneyland,

I should "pay myself" $200 first. So before every trip, I'd jump online and buy an equal amount of silver or gold.

That ritual became a personal system: *for every dollar spent on lifestyle, match it with a dollar on asset-building.*

It wasn't about getting rich off silver. It was about rewiring my brain. I stopped seeing spending as pure drain and started pairing it with investment. I was creating a rule that preserved future value every time I consumed in the present.

Looking back, it was a primitive system. But the principle still holds: build rules that force you to save, stack, and invest, *especially when you're spending.* That's what turns chaos into discipline, and discipline into leverage.

The Corporate Breakthrough

Our systems held up under pressure, but then they went on to unlock corporate doors.

In 2017, FlashPants won the season finale of *The Gong Show*, watched by three million viewers. It was hard not to be starstruck: Mike Myers, donning prosthetics to make him look like a British TV host, waited for his cues backstage; the judges—Isla Fisher, Courteney Cox, and Will Arnett—looked impassive. Inside, I wasn't sure if we'd win. Outside, we were a crimson crew of mustachioed musicians, ready to rock. The score? Perfect 10s.

That wasn't luck. It was years of brand clarity, system discipline, and scale readiness. We'd built a machine.

Chapter 7 Activity: Your Chaos-to-Machine Evaluation

Time to spot the chaos in your world and start turning it into systems that scale.

Your task: Walk through this four-step machine-building analysis. Define your brand, locate the chaos, practice systematic leadership, and design your first cloneable system.

Step 1: Brand Definition Analysis

Current Brand Audit

- What do people instantly think when they hear your name?

- What are your "red shorts and mustaches", the quirky, memorable detail that makes you stand out?
- What's the common experience people have working with you?
- What signature style or approach do others always mention about you?
  - If unsure, reach out to people who will give you honest feedback.

Brand Clarity Check

- Where are you inconsistent in how you show up?
- What could be sharper, more distinctive, or easier to recognize?
- How could you make your value unmistakable at first glance?
- What bold "Shake Weight" experiments could you test to discover brand stickiness?

Step 2: Chaos Identification

Current Chaos Inventory

- Which activity feels like "starting from zero" every time?
- Where are you the single point of failure for results?
- What would break if you disappeared for a week?
- Where are you repeating tasks that could be automated?

Impact Evaluation

- Which chaotic process drains you the most?
- Where would systematization save the most time or stress?
- Which system would free others to perform better if it existed?
- What chaos is costing you opportunities because no system supports it?

Step 3: "Leading from Behind" Practice

Audit Your Leadership Style

- Are you trying to be the hero, or are you building systems that work without you?
- What tasks could others handle if supported by good processes?
- Are you creating ownership, or just issuing commands?
- Where could you lead by clearing obstacles instead of controlling every detail?

This Week's Leadership Experiment

- Choose one area where you're currently doing everything.

- Define the outcome, not the exact procedure.

- Give someone else room to contribute their strengths.

- Focus on removing friction instead of micromanaging steps.

Step 4: Creation of Your First Cloneable System

System Selection

- Pick one process that always requires your direct involvement.

- Choose something important enough to matter, but simple enough to systematize quickly.

- Select a process others could benefit from if it were reproducible.

System-Building Steps

1. **Document**: Write down every step you currently take.

2. **Identify**: Separate what's essential from what's just habit.

3. **Framework**: Build a repeatable process others can follow.

4. **Test & Iterate**: Run it once, refine, and improve until it holds.

Examples of Cloneable Systems

- Meeting prep and follow-up

- Client onboarding and communication

- Training or instructional routines

- Project tracking and deadline monitoring

- Quality-control or review workflows

The Van Conversion System

By 2018, FlashPants was running on autopilot. Shows were steady, systems were humming, and for the first time in years, I had extra time on my hands. At first, I filled it with workouts. But something more important, more personal, was in my mind almost daily: a friend of mine was experiencing homelessness. I couldn't stomach the thought of her living on the street.

So I put two and two together. What if I could convert a minivan into a house on wheels? Nothing fancy, just functional. A bed. A refrigerator. A microwave. A sink. Storage. Fans. Even solar power.

I ordered a book on how to design your own solar battery system and got to work. My Urban Workshop classes from a few years earlier, wood shop, metal shop, welding, suddenly paid off. I cut wood, rigged metal brackets, wired solar panels, and built a simple but effective mobile home. It worked. My friend had shelter.

That project snowballed into a short-lived side hustle. I converted a few more vans, thinking it could become a business. The problem? The people who needed the vans most were the least able to pay. I couldn't scale it sustainably, but I made a real difference in a few lives.

The bigger lesson? Systems thinking isn't just for companies or bands. It's for life. When you stack skills, manual, technical, empathetic, you can turn chaos into something functional, even lifesaving.

The Resin Systems Experiment

I launched a small side business called Custom Resin Art. I'd take striking images, mount them to hand-built wood frames (thanks to skills I picked up at Urban Workshop), then pour clear resin to seal them under a glass-like finish, think the Jurassic Park mosquito in amber.

The process mattered as much as the product. I mapped each step in a CRM, cutting, mounting, first pour, air bubble removal, cure time, sanding, second pour, dust-free enclosure, finish work, delivery, so I always knew exactly where every piece sat in the pipeline. It was the FlashPants backend, translated into a studio: batching, checklists, timestamps, quality gates.

I wasn't the original artist; I've never drawn more than stick figures. My role was different: take something already good and make it unmissable. Turn raw material into a finished piece that outlived the moment it was created.

Side Lesson: The Enhancer Archetype

Not everyone has to be a visionary. Some of us are *enhancers*. We systematize, refine, and elevate. That's a legitimate power stack:

- **Manual skill** (woodworking, resin technique)

- **Process discipline** (CRM stages, dust control, curing timelines)

- **Quality amplification** (turn "great" into "gallery-ready")

Enhancers win in any field: they make teams reliable, products repeatable, and art durable. Creativity scales when someone builds the system that protects it.

Wrapping It Up

The difference between chaos and machine isn't talent. It's systems. FlashPants didn't win because we were the most musically gifted band in California. We won because we built systems where talent could scale, where creativity and structure lived side by side, and where quality could be replicated across multiple teams.

The same applies whether you're building a company, raising a family, or leading a community project. The core principles never change: a clear brand, organized processes, servant leadership, and structures that scale. The goal isn't to sterilize the human element, it's to create frameworks that let the human element shine consistently and grow sustainably.

Start small. Systematize one messy process. Build one cloneable structure. Prove it works, then repeat. The line between a stressed-out operator and a scaling leader is simple: in one world, everything depends on you. In the other, machines keep running whether you're in the room or not.

Now that you've seen how to turn chaos into a machine, it's time to explore an unexpected crucible for transferable skills: the healing arts—and how they shape leadership presence in entirely different arenas.

CHAPTER 8
THE FORK

*The curious paradox is that when I accept myself just as I am,
then I can change.*

—Carl Rogers

In 2012, I hit a fork in the road.

One path led toward becoming a professional healer. The other, becoming a professional entertainer.

I chose entertainment. But the healing skills I picked up that summer never left me. They've been imbued into everything since—band leadership, entrepreneurship, teaching, even quiet moments with friends.

After a breakup cracked me open, I didn't distract or numb myself. I saw it instead as a crucible, as an opportunity to understand myself more clearly and come back stronger. I looked inward, into the body, into breathwork.

I dove headfirst into breathwork facilitation—what is essentially the practice of using your breathing patterns to control your body's relaxation state. I also turned to energy practices, intuitive touch therapy, emotional anchoring, and pranayama (think: breath-based yoga). This wasn't about chasing some spiritual fad. It was about self-discovery. I needed answers.

I studied with David Elliott, a well-known healer who uses cyclical breathwork to unlock emotional release. In group sessions, I watched people hit emotional walls: clenched fists, shaking bodies, tears giving way to screams.

Sometimes my job was simply to sit with them silently and steadily so they felt safe enough to open up. Other times, a light hand on their shoulder or ankle grounded them while they let out waves of emotions.

It was a jarring experience, seeing humanity without the masks of job titles, status, or social context. And I learned to be present in moments most people run from. That was my initiation into unmasked empathy—not pity, not fixing—but acknowledging pain as something real.

It didn't just train me to read expressions. I stopped just looking at faces and started reading the micro-tensions in their bodies—the language of stress, grief, and repression spelled out in their posture and movements. It rewired how I understood people altogether. I stopped hearing only the words someone spoke, sensing, also, what was unsaid.

That summer taught me something I didn't yet have words for: a good healer was often also a natural leader.

The Silent Farm Crucible

After I gave up my apartment following my exit from real estate, I spent two weeks on a silent retreat with a monk named Norm Rosenberg and his cloistered partner, Tisha, on their property called Pangea Farm in upstate New York.

The days followed a rhythm I had never known before: morning meditations, more meditation after meals, and stretches of silence that sunk into my bones. Those moments were framed by a lot of manual labor—pulling weeds, trimming hedges, and cleaning the bathroom.

Tisha sometimes did bodywork and energy work with me, guiding me to notice where in my body my old emotions were stored. Norm, on the other hand, taught through film. At night we'd watch movies—*Cabaret* was one I'll never forget—and afterward, he would ask pointed questions that cut deeper than any lecture.

Time seemed not to exist—no calls, no emails, no interruptions. Meditating and journaling set the rhythm of life.

Stripped of noise, I realized how much of my so-called "urgency" was self-created. For two weeks, I experienced what life felt like when it was simply lived—moment to moment, without distractions.

When it was time to leave, I hugged Tisha goodbye and she cried softly. Norm stood steady, smiling in that grounded way he always did. Norm passed away in 2015, but that time at Pangea Farm remains one of the most peaceful, transformative seasons of my life.

On the taxi ride back to the airport, I could feel the outside world creeping back in. By the time I landed, I was back to "normal life." But the imprint lingered—stillness, quiet, emotional honesty, connection.

A Unique Library for a Deeper Purpose

During this season, I built what became one of my most prized possessions: a massive personal library. Not of business books—of healing texts.

I hunted down out-of-print volumes with yellowed pages, covering energy work, nutritional healing, plant medicine, even pre–Civil War medical manuals were part of my storehouse.

What might have looked like casual curiosity was much more than that. I was searching for answers I wasn't sure existed.

My mother's health was the spark. She'd had a heart attack when I was young, and it sent me on a quest for alternative means of healing.

Watching my mother navigate complex health challenges taught me that these challenges are not a decree you can impose from the outside. She had her own relationship with her body, her own pace of recovery, her own way of processing what was happening to her. I couldn't fix her completely but I could show up, learn everything I could, and support her on her own terms.

That distinction mattered. The books I collected were about me learning to be present with suffering I couldn't control. They taught me that sometimes love looks like acceptance rather than intervention, that respecting someone's autonomy is a form of care. I'm grateful that my desperate search for answers taught me to honor her process instead of trying to override it.

The Fork in the Road

When FlashPants started to take off, I hit another fork in the road. On one side, healing practices. On the other hand, show business.

I was booking private breathwork sessions. Guiding people through break-throughs. Getting paid for it. There was a future where I could've gone all in—professional healer, full-time energy worker.

But healing took its toll. Sitting with someone's grief, rage, numbness poured into my body.

Graysen saw it. After one pizza shift, he pulled me aside.

"Look," he said. "You gotta choose between healing or the band. FlashPants is gaining momentum."

The question took me by surprise. But I immediately knew he was right. FlashPants was exploding in popularity, and the business, like an infant, demanded my full attention. Being a healer meant living inside other people's pain every day, sometimes hours per day.

I chose the band.

Still, I kept the *healer* with me—on stages, in classrooms, in boardrooms.

Skill Alchemy

That reframe allowed me to see a boardroom or sales meeting as a healer: I immediately sensed where the other parties were coming from. An expression or body posture or turn of phrase could unwittingly signal whole icebergs of emotion. The same patterns for grounding and self-soothing worked to center me before a big meeting or presentation. My friends, employees, and clients saw the difference in my energy.

FlashPants, instead of stifling my skills as a healer, showcased them. Weddings, corporate events, quinceañeras, memorials were infused with healing skills. At one fan's memorial, I met with the family beforehand. I could feel their grief in the way they spoke—heavy, broken, longing. On stage, I steered the energy with intuition: starting reverent, then lifting the room with joy until the sadness gave way to laughter, memory, and release.

That was when I realized performance could heal. Music wasn't just noise—it was alchemy. More than once, I'd be on a break between sets and someone would pull me aside and say, *"I was gonna kill myself tonight, but I decided to come out to the bar beforehand. I saw you guys and I changed my mind… so thank you."*

Those moments hit harder than any TV appearance or packed venue.

Those moments reminded me that the healer never left. He just wore different clothes: presence instead of therapy, stagecraft instead of ritual, listening instead of diagnosis.

In 2023, I sat with a student fighting cancer. He broke down in my office: fear, family, regrets, all of it pouring out. I didn't fix it. I didn't rush him. I just listened, steady, letting him create space for his own strength to surface.

Chapter 8 Activity: Your Healer's Toolkit Inventory

Time to sharpen your energy reading, holding space, empathy, and emotional regulation skills. These aren't "soft skills." They're high-leverage human skills that will make you more effective everywhere—from business to parenting to leadership.

Your task: Complete this four-step inventory.

Step 1: Practice Reading Energy

This Week's Experiment: Pick three different conversations (work, family, friends). Before, during, and after, practice reading the energy.

Before talking, observe:

- What's the overall energy in the room?
- What do body language and micro-expressions reveal?
- What does tone, pacing, and volume tell you?
- What feels unsaid or under the surface?

While communicating, notice:

- When does the energy shift—lighter, heavier, more tense, more open?
- What topics build connection vs. trigger resistance?
- When do they feel truly heard vs. when do they feel rushed?

Afterward, reflect:

- What stayed unspoken?
- How did reading energy change your approach?
- What would you adjust next time?

Step 2: Holding Space vs. Fixing Assessment

Check your fixing reflex:

- Do you jump in with solutions the second someone shares a problem?
- Do emotions (crying, anger, fear) make you uncomfortable?
- Do you rush to console instead of letting them process?
- Do you take on others' emotions instead of holding clear space?

Holding Space practice (try this once this week):

- Give undivided attention without multitasking.
- Say: *"That sounds really hard"* instead of *"Here's what you should do."*
- Notice the urge to fix—and pause.
- Ask: *"What do you need right now?"*

Reflection:

- When do you truly hold space vs. when do you jump in to repair?
- Why is it uncomfortable to sit with someone else's raw emotion?
- How can you stay present without absorbing their energy?

Step 3: Build Your Emotional Regulation Toolkit

Audit your current state:

- How do you ground yourself when others are emotional?
- Where do you lose composure?
- What do you do to stay present vs. when you get overwhelmed?

Choose 2–3 tools to develop:

- **Breathing:** Box breathing, slow exhales.
- **Grounding:** Feet planted, notice body sensations.
- **Boundaries:** Visualize a bubble of light around yourself.
- **Centering phrases:** *"I can hold space without fixing." / "Their emotions are not mine." / "Observe; don't absorb"*.

Daily practice:

- Use one tool before tough conversations.
- Apply one tool during a stressful moment.
- Reflect nightly: What worked? What didn't?

Step 4: Integration of Healing Skills

At work (choose one):

- Team meetings → read the room before launching the agenda.
- Client relations → tune into what they need, not just what they say.

- Tough conversations → let resistance breathe before pushing back.
- Presentations → adjust delivery based on audience energy.

At home (choose one):
- Family dynamics → practice energy reading.
- Friendships → hold space without rushing to solutions.
- Conflict resolution → regulate instead of reacting.
- Parenting → read the need behind behavior.

Integration plan:
- Pick ONE healing skill to focus on for the next month.
- Define 2–3 real situations where you'll apply it.
- Track what you notice: energy shifts, reactions, outcomes.
- Adjust your approach week to week.

Bottom line: Healing skills aren't "extra." They're force multipliers. Learn to read, hold, empathize, and regulate—and you'll perform at a higher level in every arena of life.

Wrapping It Up

The healing path didn't fail just because I didn't hang a shingle as a professional healer. It became part of my stack. Nothing is wasted—not heartbreak, not detours, not the side roads that don't end in a career. Sometimes you only walk far enough down a path to grab the tools you'll need for a future you can't see yet.

The energy reading I practiced in breathwork sessions now makes me a sharper, more compassionate teacher in trading classrooms. The holding space I did for grieving clients makes me a better business partner and friend. The emotional regulation I built while managing others' pain keeps me steady during high-stakes performances and negotiations.

That's the point: all skills are transferable if you know where to look.

You don't need to be a healer to practice healer abilities. You don't need to be a therapist to cultivate therapeutic presence. Every single human interaction is a chance to read energy, hold space, and respond with wisdom instead of reactivity.

Those skills will elevate everything else you do—not because you're running around trying to fix people, but because you're attuned to what's really happening beneath the surface.

Now that you've seen how healing skills stack into leadership and business success, it's time to explore another unexpected crucible: the dance floor. Because learning to calibrate in real-time with a partner teaches you the kind of leadership you can't fake—leading without forcing, inviting without controlling, and creating flow instead of friction.

CHAPTER 9
THE DANCE FLOOR LABORATORY

*Leadership is practiced not so much in words as in attitude
and in actions*

—Harold Geneen

When John Frank Stevens arrived as chief engineer to the Panama Canal project, he did something strange. He stopped digging.

You see, the French had already tried making a canal by clawing through the humid thicket of jungle and swamp in an effort to connect two oceans. Instead, they lost *tens of thousands* of men to illnesses and accidents. To simplify a bit of history: the French eventually gave up, and the Americans took over the doomed project.

Instead of barking new orders, Stevens walked the length of the canal zone. He stood at the edge of the Culebra Cut and watched whole mountainsides of earth swallow tracks and machines. He didn't try to force his men to power through the muck.

That's what the French did—and why they failed.

Stevens's railroad engineers explained the trouble with transport, making excavation almost impossible. His doctors pointed out all the causes of yellow fever and malaria killing their men by the wagonful. His foremen groaned about the downright awful living conditions in the jungle. And guess what?

He actually listened.

He realized that the project wasn't failing because workers were lazy. It wasn't working because nobody would listen to the guys on the ground.

Rather than forcing the project, Stevens invited his men to provide boots-on-the-ground solutions. Engineers came up with gravity-fed locks for ships. Doctors helped clean up the water supply and put nets around the cabins. Yes, the project slowed down for a time. But things picked up.

Eventually, the project that many people considered impossible was finally complete. 100 years later, it's the most trafficked cargo canal in the world.

Stevens's genius was realizing that the project didn't need more muscle or another crack of the whip; it needed smart leadership.

*
**

In this chapter, you'll learn how partner dancing (of all things) became a laboratory for real-time leadership.

How I Learned to Lead with Trust

In 2017, a breakup knocked me flat. Restless, lonely, and hungry for connection—real connection—I went a-looking. I wasn't hounding random bars; I scoped one out that I actually was drawn to. Country music had always called me: raw, twangy, and alive. So one night, I walked into *InCahoots* in Fullerton, California—and it hit me like a freight train.

The energy was electric. Music thumping, boots sliding, laughter cutting through the air. Every night started with free country dance lessons, and the floor lit up with two-step, spins, and line dances. It wasn't just dancing—it was connection. Timing. Trust. Leadership. Something deep inside me said: *I don't want to watch. I want to learn.*

That's how I met Terena, the purple-haired instructor running the lessons. I asked if she taught private sessions. She said yes.

So we started meeting weekly. At first, I thought two-step was about memorizing steps and counting beats, but Terena quickly shattered that illusion. She taught me that dancing wasn't about patterns. Rather, it was about reading the energy of your partner.

A talented dance lead doesn't drag his partner across the floor (it's called a *partner* and not a *dictator* for good reason). He listens. Connection isn't force; it's tension and space. A subtle move of the hand means *rotate left*. A gentle opening of your posture: *move forward*. No yanking. No commands. No shouting. Just presence and suggestion.

One night I picked Luke Bryan's *Out of Nowhere Girl* for practice, thinking Terena might laugh at the choice. She did—and then she lit up. We flowed across the floor with no rigid counts, just music and energy. Her smile pulled me out of my head. I could *feel the trust,* the unspoken flow of our movements.

And that's the deeper lesson: on the dance floor, the lead protects the follow. Physically, emotionally, socially. If she stumbles, you catch her. If someone bumps into you, you shield her. If the floor is crowded, you navigate the traffic. Her safety—her experience—is literally in your hands. Leadership in two-step is full accountability. You're not in charge to dominate—you're in charge to guide, honor, and create something beautiful together.

Pain, Presence, and the Dance Floor Blueprint

Make no mistake: this didn't start from joy. It started from heartbreak. That breakup left me reeling. Some days, I'd pace around my apartment in silence. It was a rough time.

But if that breakup hadn't happened, I wouldn't have gone looking to bounce back; I wouldn't have met Terena. I wouldn't have discovered a whole new arena of connection, leadership, and trust.

Within months, I wasn't just passable—I became an expert two-step lead. I could guide total beginners or seasoned pros, adjusting on the fly to styles, skill levels, and personalities. Every dance was its own crucible: reading a stranger's comfort level, calibrating pressure and pace, making them feel safe, powerful, graceful—even when they were nervous inside.

I'd spot a hesitant woman at the bar, eyes darting. "Don't worry, I can teach you quick." In the corner, I'd give a turbo tutorial: *Quick-quick, slow-slow, inside turn, outside turn, keep the distance.* Then we'd hit the floor. As a drummer, I could move my body while counting rhythm out loud: *quick-quick, slow-slow.* More than once, I heard: "That counting really helped!" It wasn't about flash. It was about presence.

Two-stepping taught me what no boardroom could:

- **Calibration** — knowing when to push, pull, or hold steady.
- **Presence** — full awareness of another's experience while leading.
- **Responsibility** — owning outcomes without blaming the partner.
- **Adaptability** — adjusting in real time to a crowded floor, awkward footing, or nerves.

These lessons didn't stay on the dance floor. They followed me everywhere: business meetings, sales calls, negotiations, teaching finance classes, public speaking. Anytime I had to lead—with ideas, energy, or momentum—the blueprint came from the dance floor.

Because leadership isn't about control. It's about invitation with accountability.

I learned that by leading dozens of women across crowded floors night after night—trusting them to respond, earning their trust in return. I even started teaching couples. Guys eager to nail the lead, women learning to follow. I'd frame it like this: *It's a conversation, not a command.* Watching them sync, watching the guy's confidence grow as the woman relaxed into the rhythm—it showed me leadership isn't about making yourself look good. It's about making others shine.

Reinvention Skill Highlight: Lead with Trust

Connection isn't luck—it's a skill you can train. Here's how to stack it:

- **Step Up Clumsy:** Try something new—dance, a class, anything. Commit once this week.

- **Feel the Vibe:** Watch someone's body language. What are they saying without words?

- **Invite, Don't Force:** Lead with a suggestion, not control. Notice the difference in flow.

- **Own the Floor:** Take responsibility for one interaction's outcome—steer, don't blame.

- **Count the Rhythm:** Guide someone new with clear cues, like counts in a dance. Safety first.

The Hidden Skill Recognition

What shocked me was how fast I leveled up. In months, I wasn't just decent—I was one of the best two-step leads in the room. Why? Because my whole life had been training me for it without me realizing.

- **Timing Mastery:** Decades of drumming hardwired me to feel rhythm instinctively. I didn't think in beats—I let my body follow them naturally.

- **Real-Time Calibration:** Just like adapting to different musicians on stage, I could read each partner's comfort level and shift instantly.

- **Leading from the Ground Up:** Drumming taught me foundation. Dance demanded the same—lay down a steady base so your partner could shine.

- **Pressure Sensitivity:** Years of dynamics—when to hit hard, when to hold back—translated perfectly into the subtle push-pull of partner dance.

The skills were already there. I just had to see the transfer.

The Laboratory in Action

Every dance became a live lab experiment: reading micro-signals, adjusting in real time, building trust.

- Tension in their hands? Simplify. Slow down.

- Eyes lighting up? Push—add a spin, try a new move.

- Hesitation creeping in? Encourage. Smile. Lock eyes. Say, "You've got this."

- Fatigue showing? Shift to easier steps. Keep the connection alive.

The dance floor became my calibration lab. Every night, dozens of experiments. Every partner, a new data set. Every song, a new chance to test, refine, and lead with trust.

The Father Connection Full Circle

Looking back, I can trace this entire skill stack to my father's guitar. He never set out to teach me leadership, timing, or presence, but that's exactly what I absorbed sitting cross-legged on the carpet, staring at his hands glide across the fretboard.

He showed me that music isn't just sound—it's connection. It's pauses between phrases that give space for beauty. It's switching from complex riffs to simple melodies that make people feel good. It's looking up mid-song, catching someone's eye, and letting them know the music is a shared moment, not a performance.

For my 10th birthday, I made my friends sit on the floor and watch him play. I didn't have the words for it then, but I felt it: music could gather people, hold them, and change the room's energy.

That ethic carried into my drumming career and exploded even further on the dance floor. The beat, the rhythm, the trust… it was all seeded by those early hours of listening and watching. My father wasn't just playing guitar. He was modeling presence.

Recently, I produced a documentary on his guitar and music life as a gift to him and to myself. Growing up, he was busy providing, and I wanted him to have the chance to tell his story, guitar in hand. That film was proof: the most powerful skills often come from the most unexpected places.

How Dance Floor Skills Transfer Everywhere

Sales and Client Relations

- Reading prospect energy and adjusting in real time
- Building trust through presence, not pressure
- Leading conversations toward mutual benefit
- Knowing when to advance and when to pause

Example: A financial planner senses when clients are nervous about risk and slows down the pitch, shifting to reassurance before moving forward.

Team Management and Leadership

- Providing a steady foundation others can build on
- Calibrating in real time to individual team needs
- Leading through invitation rather than domination
- Taking responsibility for outcomes, not just directives

Example: A manager adapts communication style (step-by-step detail for one team member, top-level vision for another) while keeping everyone aligned.

Parenting and Family Dynamics

- Reading emotional cues beneath behavior
- Guiding decisions through connection, not control
- Creating safety within clear structure
- Teaching by demonstration, not force

Example: A parent notices their child is withdrawn after school and opens space to talk rather than demanding answers—building trust and modeling emotional intelligence.

Public Speaking and Education

- Reading the room's energy and adapting delivery
- Building rapport through timing, presence, and pacing
- Leading audiences through a journey rather than dumping content
- Flexing to different learning styles in real time

Example: A conference speaker senses attention fading, shifts to an interactive exercise, and brings the audience back into the experience.

Chapter 9 Activity: Your Dance Floor Laboratory

It's time to take the lessons from the floor—invitation, calibration, rhythm—and test them in your own leadership. This exercise will help you shift from control to trust, from force to invitation, and from blind spots to presence.

Step 1: Force vs. Invitation Analysis

Current Force Tendencies

- Where are you pushing people instead of inviting them?
- When do you default to "command mode" and wonder why the energy dies?
- Think of a recent situation where you forced an outcome—what could an invitation have created instead?

Invitation Practice This Week

- Choose one conversation where you'll deliberately practice leading by invitation.
- Replace "You should…" with "What if we considered…?"
- Swap orders for questions: "What feels right to you?"
- Give direction as guidance, not commands.

Step 2: Real-Time Calibration

Existing Blind Spots

- When do you miss signals that someone's overwhelmed or disengaged?
- Where do you push harder when you should pull back?

- Which micro-expressions, tone changes, or energy shifts do you usually ignore?

Calibration Practice

- In three conversations this week, pause mid-stream and assess: What's their energy telling me?

- Ask, "How does this feel?" or "What's your sense of this?"

- Notice when their words don't match their body language.

- Experiment with adjusting your pace—slowing down, speeding up, or simplifying.

Step 3: Hidden Foundation Mapping

Your dance floor calibration comes from hidden places. Time to map yours.

Questions to Ask:

- Childhood: What did your parents, environment, or early hobbies teach you about timing, connection, or trust?

- Hobbies: Which "fun" skills (sports, music, gaming, crafts) secretly trained you in rhythm, focus, or flow?

- Survival: What did hard times teach you about reading people or adapting quickly?

- Roles: Which "unrelated" jobs gave you people skills you've undervalued?

Transfer Test:
 For each, ask:

- How could this skill apply to leadership?

- Where does it give me an unfair advantage?

- What problem right now could it help me solve?

Step 4: Practice Your Lab
Select Your Lab:

- **Professional:** Team meetings, client calls, presentations

- **Personal:** Family dynamics, relationship conversations, friendships

- **Community:** Volunteering, neighborhood groups, projects

- **Learning:** Mentoring, coaching, teaching

Protocol:

- **Before:** Set the intention to lead by invitation, not force.
- **During:** Calibrate in real time—adjust pressure, timing, and energy.
- **After:** Reflect on how the interaction shifted because of presence, not pressure.

Weekly Progression:

- **Week 1:** Focus on spotting force vs. invitation in your behavior.
- **Week 2:** Build sensitivity to micro-signals and energy shifts.
- **Week 3:** Practice owning outcomes without micromanaging.
- **Week 4:** Blend all skills into your personal leadership rhythm.

Wrapping It Up

Your most important skills won't always come from classrooms, jobs, or certifications. Often they're forged in heartbreak, risk, and stepping onto unfamiliar floors. Leadership isn't volume. It's rhythm. It's felt presence. It's calibration—one small adjustment, one trusted connection, one step at a time.

Every conversation is a dance. Every meeting is a lab for trust. Every relationship is a chance to invite rather than control. Your next breakthrough may not require a new skill—it may come from recognizing what you already have and applying it differently.

And never forget: sometimes the strongest leadership move is choosing not to lead—stepping back, creating space, and letting the right opportunities move toward you.

CHAPTER 10
THE SAILOR'S COMPASS

The intuitive mind is a sacred gift and the rational mind is a faithful servant

—Albert Einstein

Evan hated improvising. He was known at the firm for being Mr. Data—checklists, models, forecasts. If a decision mattered, Evan wanted data on it (preferably in a spreadsheet).

So when his manager asked him to lead a client negotiation on short notice, Evan panicked.

"I haven't reviewed the numbers nearly enough," Evan said. "I don't have time to build scenarios."

"You've been on this account for two years," his manager replied. "You got it."

Evan spent the night building slides anyway.

The meeting went sideways fast.

Five minutes in, the client started pushing for things that didn't make sense on paper. Evan tried to slow the conversation down by pulling up slides and explaining the data. But the energy in the room had shifted. The client wasn't confused. They were probing.

In a panic, mid-sentence, Evan stopped and closed the laptop.

"I think we're talking past each other," he said. "Help me understand what problem you're trying to solve."

The room went quiet. The client leaned back, shocked. "Honestly, we're under heavy pressure from our competitors. We don't really need a discount—we need to know this won't blow up on us."

Then it finally clicked for him: the clients didn't just care about the numbers or the spreadsheets. They wanted certainty. He adjusted the new offer on the fly, tailoring the deal as they went along.

The client wanted clear milestones. Evan promised clear milestones. They mentioned how long the meeting was going; Evan bought everyone coffee. The client wavered, but Evan took the reluctant energy in the room and turned it into confidence.

The deal closed later that afternoon.

The next morning, Evan replayed the moment in his head: He let his intuition take center stage and it paid off big time. From then on, Evan changed how he prepared. He wasn't just Mr. Data anymore. He paid close attention to the tension in conversations, to what *wasn't* being said.

He trusted his gut and closed more deals.

*
**

As Evan discovered, sometimes the hunch you can't explain is the one that changes everything. You don't need the world's permission to follow it. You don't need data models or a focus group. You just need the guts to move when something inside you says *go*.

That's why this chapter is about your inner compass**,** about listening to your deepest drives and hunches—those that point you in the direction of what you're naturally called to pursue. This kind of intuition stacking is a superpower.

The Pirate Festival Spark

In 2023, my band FlashPants was booked to play Buccaneer Days—a massive pirate festival on Catalina Island, just off the Los Angeles coast. Imagine a floating Renaissance faire: adults in full corsair gear, sword fights in flip-flops, boats stacked across the harbor. It's waterborne chaos.

We got there on the Catalina Flyer, a high-speed ferry that shrinks the trip from Newport Beach, California to Avalon, the main city on Catalina from four hours to forty-five minutes. Then we took the Cyclone Boat, a huge, uncovered speed boat to Two Harbors, where the band would be performing. Spray in my face, ocean air ripping through my chest like a reset button.

And somewhere on that ride, something inside me lit up. Not a plan. Not a strategy. Not even a full thought. Just a gut punch: "I need to take sailing lessons." No reason. No checklist. No productivity angle. Just a pull.

That's what I call *intuition stacking*: following a subtle nudge and trusting it's leading somewhere important, even when you don't know where yet.

From Intuition to Instruction

After the festival, I found a sailing instructor named Marc from Santana Sailing in Long Beach, California. Even in his profile picture, the guy looked like he lived in the wind.

I signed up for Skipper 101. Then 102. Then 103.

Soon I was on a boat every week: rigging, reading the wind, tacking, jibing. Marc would say things like, "Feel the wind," or he'd shout, "Don't fight it!" as I tugged against the force of the tide. Those words landed immediately.

Over time, I saw that sailing isn't about memorizing commands or muscling ropes. There was something subtler going on. Sailing is about sensing the cues from the wind and the tides, the skies and the sailboat. It's about developing a *feel* for the skill.

Sometimes what you need to learn a skill—especially a complex skill like sailing—is intuition. It is that unspoken sense that sits on the edge between knowledge and instinct. Plenty of people have knowledge without instinct.

There is another, deeper form of intuition: having intuition about yourself. Some people know what they're supposed to do—get a traditional job, earn a degree. But other people are called by their inner sense. As Isaac Asimov, the famed sci-fi author said, "The most exciting phrase to hear in science, the one that heralds new discoveries, is not 'Eureka!' (I found it!) but 'That's funny…'"

So too with our interests. We aren't forced to have a hobby or interest because those around us do. We don't have to pick up a specific degree or career because it's what we're "supposed to do." Rather, we can follow our innermost desires, go down the roads less taken. This kind of follow-your-nose approach guides you into yourself.

It sounds a little far-fetched. But as children we naturally pursue what makes us compelled; we ask questions out of a deep-seated curiosity; we wonder about the world and aim to make an impact in it. As we grow older, we are assaulted by the media and culture to conform. *Be realistic*, the voices say.

But those voices, despite being everywhere, are not telling us the truth. Was Einstein being realistic by pursuing his interest in physics while working as a postal clerk? Was Jimi Hendrix being realistic by pushing guitar to new heights? No, these men were decidedly *unrealistic* and that is the point.

They followed their intuition—not toward the prescribed *Eureka* but *that's funny*. And it paid off.

The Power of Stacked Skills

Here's the part most people miss: skills don't just add, they multiply.

That built-in compass I'd taken for granted became an edge on the water. Add intuition, layer in Marc's technical instruction, stack on decades of stage presence and leadership—suddenly, I wasn't "just learning to sail." I was creating a sanctuary. A networking hub. A mobile freedom vehicle. A new identity.

That's the real payoff of skill stacking. The endgame isn't *competence*. It's transformation.

A New World Unlocked

Sailing became more than boats and rigging. It became:

- A place to breathe when the world felt heavy
- A space to host friends, family, even CEOs without pretense or noise
- A reminder that freedom isn't something you buy, it's something you build
- Proof that small hunches—followed—can open doors you didn't know existed

That's the magic: one gut nudge, stacked with latent ability and a willingness to learn, and suddenly a whole new dimension of life is unlocked.

Permission vs. Forgiveness

Acting on intuition often means breaking form. You won't always have approval, consensus, or a green light. Sometimes the only way forward is to act, then clean up later. Waiting kills the signal. Leaders trust the nudge, act first, and apologize if necessary.

Chapter 10 Activity: Your Sailor's Compass Evaluation

Time to uncover your hidden compass—those gut-level, almost invisible abilities—and stack them into premium skills that can change the trajectory of your life.

Step 1: Gut Feeling Inventory

Recent Nudges You've Ignored

- What activity, talent, or possibility has pulled at you lately with no logical reason?

- Where have you thought, *"I should try this..."* but shut it down?

- What environments or hobbies give you energy just by being around them?

- Which "random" interests keep resurfacing, even if they seem impractical?

- When have you wanted to approach someone, but fear stopped you—even though your gut said yes?

Intuition Patterns

- When has your gut been right in the past, even when logic disagreed?

- What early warnings or opportunities did you sense before others caught on?

- Where do you notice shifts—subtle or obvious—before they're visible to others?

Step 2: Identification of Hidden Compass

Natural Talents You Overlook

- What do people always ask you for help with because it's "easy" for you?

- What skills have you never trained, but you're naturally good at?

- What comes so effortlessly to you that you assume it's normal for everyone?

- Where do you show instinctive ability—direction, timing, reading people, patterns?

Environmental Reading

- What small changes do you pick up first—weather shifts, moods, group dynamics, markets?

- Where do you "just know" problems or opportunities before others see them?

- What soft signals do you catch that others miss?

Step 3: Small Intuition Experiment

This Week's Test
Choose one small, low-risk action driven by intuition:

- Take a different route just because it feels right.

- Text or call the person you can't get off your mind.

- Say yes to something you've been drawn to but can't explain.

- Make a minor decision based on "feel" instead of analysis.

Track Results

- What happened when you trusted the nudge?

- Was your intuition accurate?

- How did it feel to act without overthinking?

- What would you refine next time?

Step 4: Premium Skill Mapping

Your natural abilities are the raw compass. But by stacking them with complementary technical or professional skills, you can transform them into premium skills, the kind that give you an unfair advantage in business, relationships, and life.

Here's how to think about it:

- **If your hidden strength is People/Energy Reading**
  Being able to sense moods, read a room, or pick up on micro-signals is not just intuition—it's data. Pair it with sales, leadership, counseling, or entertainment, and you've got a premium skill.

- *Premium Outcome:* You become the negotiator who always knows when to push or pull back, the manager who sees team issues before they explode, or the coach who can tune into what people aren't saying but desperately need.

- **If your hidden strength is Pattern Recognition**
  Seeing connections that others miss can look like overthinking—until you apply it to markets, strategy, or innovation. Pair it with technical fields like finance, product development, or system design, and it becomes a superpower.

- *Premium Outcome:* You can forecast trends before competitors, spot inefficiencies no one else notices, and innovate solutions that feel obvious in hindsight but groundbreaking in practice.

- **If your hidden strength is Timing/Rhythm Sense**
  Maybe you've always had a good rhythm from music or sports. When you pair that sense of timing with project management, trading, or leadership, it becomes a premium edge.

- *Premium Outcome:* You know exactly when to speed up, slow down, or pivot. In markets, it makes you an early mover. In leadership, it helps you launch projects at the perfect moment. In performance, it makes you magnetic.

Your Next Move

- Which of these natural talents do you recognize in yourself?

- Which pairing feels most exciting or relevant to your current season of life?

- What is one small, low-risk step you could take this month to test that pairing in the real world?

- Who already excels in this domain that you could learn from—or apprentice under—to accelerate your stacking?

- How could this premium skill directly serve your biggest current goals?

The point isn't to romanticize intuition—it's to engineer it into leverage. Your hidden compass, once stacked with deliberate practice and technical knowledge, becomes a premium skill set that other people will pay for, follow, and rely on.

Wrapping It Up

That nudge on the Cyclone boat wasn't random. It was my intuition recognizing an opening. I was stacking a latent strength (spatial awareness) with a new technical skill (sailing) in an environment that felt aligned. The outcome wasn't just learning to sail. It was proof that I could trust my inner compass (pun intended), and that my gut could unlock opportunities no spreadsheet ever would.

Your instincts are already pointing toward hidden abilities waiting to be developed. The question isn't *if* they're valid. The question is whether you'll act before the world gives you permission. The biggest breakthroughs often start as quiet whispers in unlikely places.

Pay attention. Act on the nudge. Tailwinds may be invisible, but they are strong enough to be felt. Trust that intuition, and you'll open doors you didn't even know existed. But remember, intuition alone doesn't scale. Scaling requires another layer of mastery: building systems that work for you, even while you sleep.

That's where we're headed next.

CHAPTER 11
THE PIVOT POINT

You can't connect the dots looking forward; you can only connect them looking backward. So you have to trust that the dots will somehow connect in your future.

—Steve Jobs

John had spent eight years building his consulting business. It had grown steadily, enjoying predictable revenue. Then a change in his industry hit: An AI-based tool wiped out many companies like his. Within six months, half of his services were obsolete.

"I don't know what to do," he confessed to his coach, Elijah. "The tools out there are doing what I used to charge $5,000 for."

Elijah leaned in. "Walk me through what you *actually* do for clients."

"I audit workflows, spot bottlenecks, design more efficient processes, and train teams to implement them."

"And *how* do you do that?"

"I interview stakeholders. I map systems. I translate complexity into simple steps people can actually follow."

Elijah smirked. "So, you can read systems, see what others miss, explain tricky problems clearly, and lead teams through change. And you think AI makes you redundant?"

John hesitated. "…when you put it like that…"

"Here's the play. Don't learn AI to compete with it. Learn it to *amplify* what you already do better than anyone else."

"But I'm not technical," John said.

"You don't need to be. You're not here to code. You're here to translate. AI can crunch data, but it can't read a company's culture, defuse resistance in a boardroom, or guide people through change. That's where you win."

John nodded. "So my edge isn't becoming an AI expert. It's being the strategist who shows businesses how to *use* AI insights to solve human problems."

"Exactly. Spend some time learning the tools that speed up your research. Then charge premium rates for doing what AI can't do—helping people act on what the tools reveal."

Within weeks, John was auditing workflows with AI, delivering insights in hours that used to take weeks. Clients weren't just impressed by the speed—they were floored by how clearly he translated the results into action.

Six months later, he'd rebranded as an AI-driven business strategist. Using the same core skills, only with a better understanding of his tools, John was able to position himself as a premium consultant.

"The real pivot," John told Elijah, "wasn't learning AI. It was realizing pattern recognition and change management don't get automated—they get *amplified*."

*
**

As John found that disruption can be the catalyst for your next evolution…

You may be looking at your current challenges as dead ends when they're really pivot points. This chapter will show you how to spot when it's time to pivot, build learning agility, and stack new capabilities on top of old ones to create something more powerful than what you lost.

When Your World Gets Erased

March 12, 2020

That's the day FlashPants died. Not forever. But long enough to feel like forever.

COVID shut down every venue. Corporate events? Gone. Weddings? Gone. Festivals? Gone. The entertainment industry hit a wall in 48 hours.

FlashPants had been my main income source for nearly a decade. Two hundred-plus shows a year. Multiple casts booked solid through the summer. Corporate clients on retainer.

Overnight, it vanished. I had two options: panic or pivot.

Here's the mistake most people make about pivots: They think it means burning the past and starting from zero. Wrong.

A pivot is taking your strongest footing and turning it in a new direction. I didn't stop being an entertainer. I didn't abandon my ability to read a room, handle pressure, or deliver results under the spotlight.

I just found a new stage.

Short or Long?

I'd been dabbling in the markets for years. I made casual bets with money I could afford to lose. But when the world closed, I suddenly had something most didn't: time.

The world ground to a halt. No rehearsals. No travel. No gigs. So instead of waiting for venues to reopen, I dove headfirst into trading.

And here's what I had going in that most beginners don't:

- **Performance under pressure** – nine years on stage conditioned me to stay calm under high-stakes moments
- **Pattern recognition** – reading the energy of a crowd translated into reading market sentiment
- **Risk management** – juggling multiple band casts taught me portfolio thinking
- **Teaching skill** – years of training band members gave me the ability to break down complex ideas

I wasn't coming in empty-handed. I already had transferable tools, I just had to learn the new rules of the game. I signed up for every course I could find. Studied for my Series 65. Read books. Watched videos. Paper-traded until the rhythm of the markets felt as natural as a drumbeat.

But here's the key: I wasn't learning from scratch. I was porting over skills.

- **Stage presence → classroom presence.** Guiding a crowd through a two-hour show felt exactly like teaching students through a tough financial concept.
- **Risk management → position sizing.** Just like I wouldn't book more gigs than we had capacity for, I wouldn't risk more capital than I could afford to lose.
- **Performance anxiety → trading psychology.** The butterflies before a sold-out show? Same feeling as the moment before a high-stakes trade.

I wasn't building a new foundation. I was building on top of the one I already had.

From Student to Teacher

Many months later, I wasn't just trading. I was teaching trading workshops—and I still do.

The same hotels that once hosted FlashPants gigs now booked the trading workshops that I would present. Same venues. Same energy. Same ability to hold a room's attention for hours. The subject matter had changed, but the core skills hadn't.

That's the truth about pivots: you don't reinvent yourself from nothing—you repurpose what you already do best.

The Four Skills Every Pivot Requires

Looking back, every successful pivot, mine and the dozens I've studied, comes down to four core skills:

1. Learning Agility

This isn't about IQ. It's about adaptability.

What it means:

- Learn new things fast
- Connect new knowledge to old experiences
- Adjust strategy based on feedback
- Stay curious instead of defensive when wrong

How to build it: Each quarter, pick one new domain and force yourself to learn it well enough to teach someone else. Notice where you stumble. That's where the real growth lives.

Example: A newlywed who quickly adapts from solo decision-making to factoring in a spouse's preferences: learning on the fly without resenting the adjustment.

2. Foundation Recognition

Most people panic in pivots because they think they're starting from zero. False.

You already have transferable skills, experiences, and relationships. The only question: can you spot them?

How to build it: After every major experience, ask: *"What did this teach me that applies somewhere else?"*

Example: Using communication skills from friendships as the foundation for marriage, instead of assuming you need to start over learning "relationship skills."

3. Bridge Building

A pivot isn't abandoning the old you. It's building a bridge from who you were to who you're becoming.

I didn't leave entertainment behind. I brought the principles of performance into education. I wasn't done being a performer, I just started performing in classrooms instead of nightclubs.

How to build it: Look for intersections between your old world and your new. That overlap is your bridge.

Example: Keeping your personal hobbies and friendships while also building shared experiences in marriage, bridging the single you with the partnered you.

4. Rapid Credibility

When you pivot, people might question your expertise. That's fine; you're new to the field. But generating early wins in your field is important for your success. Credibility is the currency of trust. Without it, others are unwilling to take you under their wing or give you opportunities. With it, countless doors will open to you.

How to build credibility:

- Lead with results. Do not emphasize titles, degrees, or certifications unless they are relevant.

- Be honest: share your method. If you're approaching a field differently than others, share your unique style.

- Document your progress. Nobody is born knowing quantum physics or Purple Rain. Everybody has to learn the basics before becoming experts. Don't hide your development.

Example: A partner who earns trust not with words but with consistent daily actions. The credibility grows from proof, not promises.

Chapter 11 Activity: Your Pivot Analysis

Time to measure your pivot readiness and chart your next move. Use this four-step framework to spot pivot points, test your agility, practice transfer, and build a strategy that minimizes risk while maximizing upside.

Step 1: Identifying Pivot Points

Start by naming the cracks in your current path and sketching out where a pivot could go.

Current Pressure Points

- What feels unsustainable long-term?

- Where are you hitting ceilings that incremental effort won't break?

- Which external forces (tech, markets, life events) are making your current path harder?

- What keeps you up at night thinking, *"this can't continue forever"*?

Potential Pivot Directions

- If you had to change careers tomorrow, what would you be curious enough to learn?

- What problems do you see that you're uniquely positioned to solve?

- Which of your talents could thrive in a different context?

- Where are there opportunities others are missing—or avoiding?

Step 2: The Learning Agility Test

Rate yourself **1–10** on each of these agility muscles:

Information Absorption

- How quickly do you pick up new information?

- How comfortable are you learning from people younger or less experienced?

- How effectively do you learn from failure without getting defensive?

Pattern Recognition

- How well do you spot connections others miss?

- How fast can you see what's working—and what's not—in new situations?

- How well do you adapt your approach based on feedback?

Curiosity Maintenance

- How energized do you feel about learning new things?
- How comfortable are you being a beginner again?
- How okay are you with not knowing the answer?

Teaching Ability

- How clearly can you explain something you've just learned?
- How well can you simplify complex ideas for others?
- How comfortable are you teaching before you're an "expert"?

Step 3: Practice Knowledge Transfer

Prove to yourself that what you learn is portable.

This Week's Activity:

Pick one thing you've learned recently and teach it to someone else. Examples:

- A new work process you figured out
- A cooking method you tested
- An idea from a book or podcast
- A problem-solving trick that worked

After Teaching, Reflect:

- What was hardest to explain?
- What questions stumped you?
- How did teaching sharpen your own understanding?
- What would you do differently next time?

Step 4: Pivot Preparation Strategy

Now stack your skills, build your bridge, and reduce the risk.

Foundation Mapping

- What are your top five transferable skills?
- Which relationships would still matter in a new context?
- What experiences do you have that most people in your target field lack?

- How could your background be a strength, not a weakness?

Bridge Building Plan

- What's one tiny experiment you can run to test interest in a new direction?
- How can you start building credibility in that area without leaving your current lane?
- What would your accelerated learning plan look like (timeline, resources, accountability)?
- Who has already made this pivot—and what can you learn from them?

Risk Mitigation

- What's the smallest possible pivot you could make to test the waters?
- How much runway (financial/emotional) do you have to support this shift?
- What do you need in place before making a bigger move?
- If it doesn't work, how could you reverse course without burning everything down?

This Activity isn't about guessing your next move—it's about engineering it. Pivots feel risky, but they're predictable when you can name your foundations, test small, and move with agility.

Wrapping It Up

When the world reopened and venues started booking again, FlashPants didn't just return—it came back stronger. The systems we'd built, the brand we'd cemented, the relationships we'd nurtured—they hadn't vanished. They'd been waiting. And my pivot into financial education hadn't distracted me from the band. It had sharpened me. I returned to the stage not just as a drummer, but as a more confident leader, teacher, and operator.

That's the truth about pivots: you don't lose your foundation—you layer on top of it. Every stage you've worked, every challenge you've endured, every crisis you've survived is raw material for the next version of you.

The real question isn't *Am I ready to pivot?* The real question is: *Am I willing to admit I've been preparing for this all along?*

Because reinvention isn't a reset. It's a revelation.

Now that we've mapped how to handle transitions while stacking existing skills, it's time to explore the art of creating space—the discipline of letting the right opportunities find you when you stop forcing and start aligning.

CHAPTER 12
THE ENTERTAINER'S EDGE

People will forget what you said, people will forget what you did,
but people will never forget how you made them feel.

—Maya Angelou

Daniel had all the credibility: an MBA from a top school and a decade of rock-solid analytics experience. When he stepped into the boardroom to pitch his restructuring plan, he was certain his airtight numbers would win the day.

Twenty minutes later, he was dying inside. The executives' eyes had glazed over around slide 12. Halfway through the presentation, they were checking phones and whispering to assistants. When Daniel finally asked, "Any questions?" The silence made the answer obvious: he'd lost them.

The deal went to his rival—a guy with half the credentials, who spoke for fifteen minutes with no slides. Just stories. Stories that made the room lean forward.

"I don't get it," Daniel told his musician friend, Jesse, later. "My analysis was stronger. My recommendations were more complete."

Jesse didn't flinch. "You used that room as a classroom instead of a stage. You delivered information instead of an experience. In business, technical ability gets you in the room. Stage presence closes the deal."

"But I'm not a performer," Daniel argued. "I'm an analyst."

"That's your problem," Jesse replied. "Every leader is a performer. You don't have to act—you have to connect. Start simple. Don't say, 'This strategy boosts efficiency by 23%.' Say, 'Picture your staff going home an hour earlier every night because this strategy removed the bottlenecks keeping them here late.' Same data. Different impact."

Daniel spent the next month practicing in front of a mirror, recording himself, dissecting TED talks like game film. His next pitch? Three slides. Twenty minutes. Two stories. And a signed contract.

"The crazy thing," he told Jesse afterward, "is I always thought performance skills were fluff. Turns out they're the only thing that made my expertise matter."

*
**

Just like Daniel, you might be undervaluing performance. You may think your work speaks for itself. But without the ability to connect, engage, and command attention, your expertise never leaves the ground. In this chapter, you'll learn the five entertainer skills that separate the ignored from the unforgettable—and how to stack them into your edge.

The Room Where Everything Changed

Sony Studios—Culver City, California

Picture this: We are the finalists on *The Gong Show* to three million viewers. I'm donning our FlashPants classic red shorts and a fake mustache. We're silently panting after our set, beads of sweat pooling from the effort and the anticipation. We had ninety seconds to impress three celebrity judges—Isla Fisher, Courtney Cox, and Will Arnett. We gave it all, but my thoughts begin to race. *Were we good enough? Did I perfectly keep the beat?* Nine years of FlashPants shows were all leading to this. What will they say?

The celebrities give us the news: Perfect 10's. We win the season finale in front of three million people. After the confetti fell and the celebration quieted, it hit me: it wasn't about the music. We were good musicians—but not world-class. Half the other acts had more technical skill.

We won because we knew something they didn't. Performance isn't about perfection. It's about connection. We made our performance unforgettable by making it personal.

The Five Skills That Dominate Every Room

FlashPants taught me that five skills determine whether you own a room—or get swallowed by it. These are not "nice to have" soft skills. They're survival skills. They decide whether people listen, follow, and trust—or tune out.

1. Stage Presence: The Ability to Command Attention

Stage presence isn't confidence. Plenty of confident people are boring. Stage presence is the ability to make everyone in the room feel like you're speaking to them directly.

What it looks like:

- You walk into a room and the energy shifts.
- People put their phones down when you speak.
- Conversations pause when you join.
- You command attention without raising your voice.

How FlashPants drilled this into me:

On stage, you get thirty seconds to hook a crowd before they drift back to their own conversations. I learned to scan faces in the front row, lock eyes, and adjust my energy to exactly what the room needed in that moment.

How it transfers:

Every conversation is a performance. Every meeting is a stage. Every sales call is an audition. Presence is the difference between being tolerated and being unforgettable.

2. Timing: The Rhythm That Makes Everything Land

Timing isn't just for comedians. It's for anyone who wants their words—or actions—to hit with maximum impact.

What it looks like:

- You pause at the right moment so your point sinks in.
- You sense when someone is ready to hear the truth vs. when they need a warm-up.
- You deliver ideas in digestible bites instead of data dumps.

- You recognize when a conversation is over and stop before it drags.

How FlashPants drilled this into me: Every song has a pocket—the groove that moves people. Play too intensely? Too fast? You lose them. Drag the pace? They get bored. I learned to match the rhythm of the room.

But timing is also about strategic interruption. Attention spans are short. Phones come out. Minds wander. That's why we dropped in the *Shake Weight competition*, the *gummy worm* bit, and even surprised everyone with *Gangnam Style* (yeah, we went there). Those weren't random gags. They were pattern interrupts, planned curveballs that reset attention and used the crowd's natural ADD in our favor.

Here's the rule: the second you see phones light up, you've got 30 seconds to win them back. That's when you hit them with something unexpected. Understand this and you don't just keep people interested—you condition them to expect the unexpected from you.

How it transfers: Every sales pitch, meeting, or tough conversation has rhythm. Master the timing and you control the tempo and the outcome.

3. Energy Management: How to Raise or Drop the Temperature

Energy management is the ability to control the emotional thermostat of a room—on purpose.

What it looks like:

- You can defuse tension without saying "calm down."
- You can inject spark into a boring meeting.
- You know when to encourage vs. when to challenge.
- You keep your own energy steady no matter what others bring.

How FlashPants drilled this into me: We played everything from drained-after-work corporate events to rowdy parties where the crowd came in already lit. Same setlist, completely different energy strategy. I learned to be a **thermostat, not a thermometer**—to set the temperature instead of reflecting it.

How it transfers: Leadership is energy management. Parenting is energy management. Sales is energy management. In every interaction, you're the tone-setter. If you can learn to raise or lower the emotional heat on demand, you're already leading.

4. Audience Reading: The Skill That Makes Everything Else Work

Audience reading is pattern recognition applied to human behavior—in real time.

What it looks like:

- You can tell within 30 seconds if someone's engaged or just being polite.
- You catch when people check out—before they even realize it.
- You sense when a group is ready to move forward vs. when they need more time.
- You adjust based on what you're seeing, not what you rehearsed.

How FlashPants drilled this into me: Wedding crowds aren't corporate crowds. Nightclubs aren't country clubs. We were the same band playing the same songs—but the micro-signals were different: eye contact, body language, and how people responded to banter. In the early days, before we had solidified the song order, choreography, and comedic skits, we had to read each crowd quickly and adjust everything—jokes, pacing, and song order—on the fly.

How it transfers: Sales calls, dates, job interviews—every one of them is a real-time calibration exercise. If you're not reading the room, you're missing it.

5. Network Building: Turning Moments into Relationships

Networking isn't stacking business cards. It's stacking moments people remember.

What it looks like:

- People introduce you because they're excited about you, not obligated.
- You stay in touch without being clingy.
- You remember details that matter to others.
- You give value before you ever ask for anything.

How FlashPants drilled this into me: Every show was networking. Club owners. Promoters. Fans who happened to be execs with deep pockets. But here's the key: I didn't network *during* the show. I made the show so unforgettable that people wanted to connect *after*. That's the ultimate pull strategy.

How it spreads: Your network is only as strong as the value you've delivered. Transactional networking dies. Value-based networking compounds. Scan the code to access the Self-Evaluation Checklist for Performance Skills

Why Technical Skills Without Performance Skills Don't Matter

I've watched brilliant consultants lose contracts to average ones who could simply tell a better story. I've seen executives ignored because they dumped data, while a competitor painted a vision people could feel.

Technical skill gets you in the room. Performance skill determines whether anyone listens once you're there.

The Network That Never Dies

I've kept every phone I've ever owned since my first Nokia in 2000—not for nostalgia, but for the contacts. Each device is a time capsule of networks: Starbucks coworkers, real estate clients, FlashPants venue owners, trading students, consulting contacts.

Most people lose their networks when they change phones or careers. I stack mine.

And here's why it matters: someone from chapter three of your life might be the key to chapter seven. The club owner you entertained in 2015 might hire you to keynote their company retreat in 2030. The real estate client you helped in 2008 might bring you into their investment group a decade later.

Your network isn't who you know *now*. Your network is your networth.

Chapter 12 Activity: Your Entertainer's Edge Inventory

Time to evaluate your performance muscles and deliberately strengthen them. This isn't about pretending to be someone you're not. It's about harnessing the same tools entertainers use to win over rooms and applying them in business, leadership, and relationships.

Your task: Complete the four-step entertainer analysis below. Audit your current skills, rehearse intentionally, and start showing up with presence every day.

Step 1: Performance Skills Audit

Rate yourself 1–10 for each category. Be brutally honest. Anything below a 7 is a growth edge.

Stage Presence

- Do people take notice when you enter a room?
- Can you command attention without raising your voice?
- Do conversations pause when you join them?
- Do people remember you after just one brief interaction?

Timing

- Do you know when to stop for emphasis rather than rambling?
- Can you sense when someone is ready to commit—or when they need more lead-in?
- Do you deliver information in bite-sized pieces instead of overwhelming with data?
- Do you know when to end a conversation before it drags?

Energy Management

- Can you cool a heated moment without saying "calm down"?
- Can you inject energy into a flat room without being corny?
- Do you maintain your own energy regardless of other people's moods?
- Can you read when to encourage vs. when to challenge?

Audience Reading

- Can you tell within 30 seconds if someone is genuinely engaged or just polite?
- Do you notice subtle disengagement before the other person realizes it?
- Do you adjust your approach on the fly instead of sticking to a rigid plan?
- Do you feel group dynamics shift in real time?

Network Building

- Do others introduce you to people with genuine enthusiasm?
- Do you follow up without being pushy or transactional?

- Do you remember details that matter to people (names, preferences, milestones)?
- Do you give value before asking for anything in return?

Step 2: Performance Practice

This week, pick one literal and one metaphorical performance drill. Don't just "think" about them—run them like reps in a gym.

Literal Performance

- Tell a story at dinner instead of just giving information. Add pauses, gestures, and tone shifts.
- Stand while pitching an idea at work—notice how posture changes authority.
- Practice a key conversation in front of a mirror to catch nervous tics.
- Record yourself explaining something, then rewatch to see where you lose energy or clarity.

Metaphorical Performance

- In one social interaction, focus 100% on the other person's engagement level—mirror their energy, adjust yours.
- Match your energy deliberately to the situation (dial down in tension, dial up in celebration).
- Use pauses strategically in your next meeting or call. Let silence do the work.
- Frame your next conversation as an *experience*, not just an exchange of info.

Reflection Questions:

- What shifted when you treated it like a performance?
- What reactions did you notice in others—positive or negative?
- Where did you have their full attention? Where did you lose it?
- What small, realistic adjustment could make you 10% more engaging next time?

Step 3: Network Audit

Contact Archaeology

Your phone is a time capsule: buried inside are countless old connections, friends, and opportunities.

- Scroll through the last five years of contacts.
- Identify 10 people you've lost touch with who once brought value—mentors, peers, collaborators, even clients.
- Note what they were doing back then and make an educated guess at where they are now.
- Pick three to re-engage with this month. Keep it agenda-free—"Hey, thought of you, how are you?"

Why this works: Opportunities don't always come from new people. Often they come from dormant ties you've ignored[1].

Network Mapping

Organize your network into five categories:

- **Career contacts**: People who know what you're capable of professionally.
- **Personal relationships**: People who'd vouch for you personally, recommend you to friends, or offer support.
- **Industry insiders**: People plugged into the trends, gossip, and opportunities before they hit the mainstream.
- **Skill mentors**: People who know what you want to learn and could accelerate your growth.
- **Collaboration partners**: People who could co-create something with you right now.

Your action: Write one name in each bucket. If a bucket is empty, that's your growth edge.

Value Creation Plan

For each person you mapped, ask yourself:

- How can I make their life easier right now?

---

1   For deeper relationship-building strategies beyond contact archaeology, Keith Ferrazzi's *Never Eat Alone* provides comprehensive frameworks for systematic networking and relationship maintenance.

- Who could I introduce them to?

- What insight, tool, or opportunity could I share?

- What problem could I help them solve?

Networking is value-first. If you're not creating opportunities, you're not building a network—you're hoarding phone numbers.

Step 4: Development of Daily Stage Presence

Daily Practices

- **Morning reset**: 2 minutes of posture + breathing. Shoulders back, chest open, grounded stance. Start the day present.

- **Conversation filter**: In every interaction, prioritize *rapport over information*. Leave people feeling better, not just informed.

- **Energy scan**: Notice your vibe. Do you need to raise energy (inject enthusiasm) or drop it (calm a tense moment)? Adjust deliberately.

- **Attention read**: Watch for signs of real engagement vs. polite nods. If you've lost them, pivot.

Weekly Challenges

- **Week 1 – Stage Presence**: Walk into every room with conscious posture, eye contact, and vocal variety.

- **Week 2 – Timing**: Practice pausing for emphasis and noticing when others lean in or zone out.

- **Week 3 – Energy Management**: Experiment with deliberately raising flat energy or calming stress in conversations.

- **Week 4 – Audience Reading**: Focus solely on engagement cues. Adapt on the fly.

Monthly Networking Rhythm

- Reconnect with 3 dormant contacts.

- Build 2 new relationships (value-first).

- Introduce 2 people who should know each other.

- Follow up with 5 priority relationships.

Do this consistently and you stop being "someone with contacts" and become "someone people remember."

Wrapping It Up

Winning *The Gong Show* wasn't about being the best band on stage. It was the culmination of six years spent mastering the five performance skills that actually move people—reading the room, managing energy, commanding attention, and creating unforgettable moments. Those skills didn't retire with the shorts and mustaches. They came with me into every sales call, every negotiation, every boardroom, every relationship.

Performance skills are what allow you to command any room. But the ultimate performer's edge isn't always in holding the spotlight. It's in knowing when to step off the stage, create space, and let the right opportunities come to you.

Next up: we'll break down the entrepreneur's formula—the five meta-skills that separate people who just work in businesses from those who build them.

CHAPTER 13
THE ENTREPRENEUR'S FORMULA

The system runs the business. The people run the system.
—Michael E. Gerber

Mary was three years into her freelance graphic design hustle. Same story every month: chase clients, crank out projects, pray the pipeline didn't run dry.

"I'm on the hamster wheel," she told her friend Lois over coffee. "When I'm working, I earn. When I stop, everything stops. There's no business here—just me trading time for dollars."

Lois leaned in. "What do your clients complain about most?"

"That's easy. They all say finding designers is a nightmare. Either the person's cheap and terrible, or they're good and booked solid. There's no middle ground."

"So you've discovered a real problem that a lot of people feel," Lois said.

"Yeah, but I can't fix an industry-wide problem. I'm just one person."

"What if you weren't?" Lois countered. "What if you created a system that paired clients with pre-screened designers who met your standards?"

"But how would I even start?"

"All businesses begin with one assumption: do people really want what you think they want? Test that before you build anything big."

"How?"

"Start small. Grab five designers you already trust. Create a lightweight vetting process—portfolio review, references, maybe a test project. Then connect them with ten clients who need exactly what you're describing. Don't overcomplicate it. See if the problem is real."

Mary got it. She reached out to five freelancers, spun up a basic one-page site with a simple form, and matched her neighbor's startup with a vetted designer named Jake. She took a $200 commission. Not much money, but it proved the concept.

Within months, word spread. Designers referred designers. Clients referred clients. Mary added a repeatable screening system—portfolio review, two references, one test project—and suddenly, she wasn't freelancing anymore.

Six months later, her "side experiment" had grown into a design marketplace with 47 vetted freelancers. Mary was earning commissions on every project without touching a design file.

"The biggest milestone," she told Lois, "wasn't becoming a better designer. It was learning to think like a business builder instead of a service provider."

*
**

Just like Mary, you might still be thinking like a freelancer when you need to be thinking like an entrepreneur. In this chapter, we'll break down the five foundational skills that separate people who *work in* businesses from people who *build* them.

The Problem That Launched Everything

In 2023, I was livid. As a marketing strategist with more client requests than I could handle, I kept seeing the same dumpster fire everywhere: businesses burning through worthless leads.

The salespeople at these companies would grow demoralized and telemarketers exhausted.

I kept watching campaigns pack their events with people who had no business being there… people who couldn't afford what was being sold, weren't actually interested, or just weren't ready to buy anything. What happened next was predictable: marketing funnels got clogged with junk leads, everyone wasted their time, and the sales team ended up sorting through a mess of unqualified prospects.

I'd built my reputation on fixing tough marketing problems—the kind that required both technical chops and creative problem-solving. My roster had a waiting list. But even the *successful* companies I consulted with had the same structural flaw: their lead generation was broken.

Marketing budgets were torched on campaigns that packed seminar rooms with dreamers who couldn't buy. CRM systems bloated with "prospects" who'd never pay a dime.

The waste wasn't just frustrating. It was offensive.

So I built a solution. YPAR—Your Perfect Audience Reach.

Our firm uses a system to pre-qualify leads before they ever hit our clients' pipeline. We do not merely generate more leads; we help them get better leads. Those are the leads that actually bring value to clients, the kind that actually close.

Most people see problems and complain. Entrepreneurs see problems and build systems that solve them. You can reach us at YPARfirm.com or by scanning the QR code above.

The Abilities Every Entrepreneur Masters

Here's the truth: entrepreneurship isn't about "great ideas." Ideas are cheap. It's about mastering five meta-skills that turn any problem into profit.

1. Problem Identification: Seeing What Others Ignore

Most people live with problems. Entrepreneurs chase them down.

What it means:

- Spotting friction others just accept as "normal"
- Hearing the same complaint from different people and knowing it's an opportunity
- Recognizing when "solutions" don't actually solve anything
- Zeroing in on problems people are *willing to pay to solve*

How it transfers outside business:

- **Family life:** Identifying recurring conflicts that need systems, not band-aids
- **Health:** Finding root causes instead of popping painkillers
- **Relationships:** Noticing toxic patterns early and dealing with them head-on

2. Solution Design: Building What Works

Forget perfection. Solutions don't need polish. They need to work.

What it means:

- Begin with the *outcome* clients actually want
- Work backward to the simplest possible path
- Test small, build big
- Iterate based on what works in the real world, not what sounds smart in a pitch deck

How it transfers:

- **Productivity:** Simple, repeatable habits that actually stick
- **Fitness:** Programs that get done, not programs that look good on paper
- **Learning:** Study methods that deliver retention, not just activity

3. Risk Management: Playing Smart, Not Safe

Smart entrepreneurs don't dodge risk. They manage it intelligently.

What it means:

- Start small to test assumptions before scaling
- Set stop-loss points so failure never wipes you out
- Build multiple income streams so no single one kills you
- Create systems that can take a hit and keep going

How it transfers:

- **Career moves:** Side hustles that test new paths without blowing up your paycheck
- **Investments:** Diversifying instead of going all-in on hype
- **Relationships:** Opening up gradually instead of betting the farm on day one

4. Team Building: Multiplying Through Others

Entrepreneurship is not doing everything yourself. It's creating leverage through people.

What it means:

- Knowing what *not* to do yourself

- Finding specialists where you're weak

- Designing systems so quality work happens without your constant supervision

- Building culture where ownership is shared and outcomes matter more than titles

How it transfers:

- **Marriage:** A partnership where each plays to strengths instead of keeping score

- **Parenting:** Teaching kids ownership instead of micromanaging every move

- **Community:** Running groups where everyone has a role that matters

- **Workplace:** Teams that function without bottlenecking through "the boss"

5. Systems Creation: Building Machines That Run Themselves

This is the line in the sand between a freelancer and a true entrepreneur. If your business only works when you're in the room, you don't have a business—you have a job.

What systems creation really means:

- Documenting processes so others can replicate them without guesswork

- Automating repetitive tasks so your brain is freed up for higher-value problems

- Installing quality-control checkpoints that catch mistakes early, before they compound

- Building feedback loops that continuously improve performance over time

How it transfers outside business:

- **Household management:** Create habits and routines that run without constant decisions (meal prep, bill pay, family calendars)

- **Financial habits:** Subscribing yourself to a financial newspaper to be more informed about the markets.

- **Skill development:** Build practice systems (daily reps, tracking, review) that ensure consistent progress instead of random effort

Why Most "Entrepreneurs" Fail

"Entrepreneurs" skip steps; they race into solution design without ever validating the real problems; they hide from risk instead of managing it; they try to do everything solo instead of building teams; they create glorified jobs for themselves instead of real companies.

Michael Gerber nailed this in *The E-Myth Revisited*: most small businesses fail because the founder works in the business, not on the business.

Real entrepreneurs understand that busywork is the enemy of what they should be doing: solving problems at scale. Scan the code to access the Framework for Identifying and Solving Business Problems

The Entrepreneur Test

Want to know if you actually think like an entrepreneur? Ask yourself:

- What problems do you hear people complain about again and again?
- Where are "solutions" just band-aids that don't fix anything?
- If failure wasn't permanent, what would you build?
- Who could help you build it better than you could alone?
- What's the smallest, cheapest version you could test this month?

If you can't answer, you're not ready yet. If you can, you're already ahead of 90% of the people out there calling themselves entrepreneurs.

For frameworks on testing systematically, Eric Ries's *The Lean Startup* is the playbook for lean experiments. Jim Collins's *Good to Great* dives into systems thinking that creates organizations built to last beyond their founders.

Chapter 13 Activity: Your Entrepreneur Formula Assessment

Time to evaluate your business-building skills and start thinking like a problem-solver.

Step 1: Problem Identification Practice

This Week's Hunt:

- What do your co-workers complain about constantly?

- What frustrations do friends vent about regularly?

- What inefficiencies do you see in everyday systems?

- What "solutions" exist that don't actually work?

Problem Quality Test:
For every problem you spot, ask:

- Do multiple people share this problem?

- Are they already spending money to fix it (poorly)?

- Would they pay more for something that actually works?

- Can you think of a simpler way to solve it?

Step 2: Risk Management Assessment

Rate yourself (1–10).

Risk Identification:

- How good are you at spotting negatives before they happen?

- Do you set clear limits on what you're willing to lose?

- Do you know the difference between gambling and calculated risk?

Risk Mitigation:

- Do you test small before going big?

- How well do you build multiple options instead of betting everything on one?

- Can you pivot quickly when something isn't working?

Step 3: Development of Small System

This Month's Project:
Create one small system that solves a recurring problem in your life.

Examples:

- Automate bill payments to avoid monthly decision fatigue
- Develop a meal-prep routine that minimizes daily food decisions
- Build an exercise habit that runs without motivation
- Establish a lightweight networking system that maintains relationships automatically

System Success Criteria:

- Works without your daily attention
- Produces repeatable results
- Can be transferred to someone else
- Improves over time with feedback

Step 4: Problem-to-Solution Pipeline

Make your opportunity map.

Current Issues You Might Solve:

- What do you instinctively solve for friends/family?
- What inefficiencies drive you crazy that others tolerate?
- What are you skilled at that would solve common frustrations?

Solution Possibilities:

- What's the simplest solution to each issue?
- Who else has this problem?
- What would they pay for a working fix?
- How could you test it this month?

Next Steps:

1. Pick one issue to focus on.
2. Design the simplest possible solution.
3. Find one person willing to test it.

4. Set clear limits on time and money.

Wrapping It Up

This is the entrepreneur formula:

1. Spot real problems.

2. Create simple solutions.

3. Manage risk smartly.

4. Build teams intentionally.

5. Develop systems that run without you.

The formula doesn't change—only the context does. Whether you're building a company, optimizing your health, or managing a family, the same five skills apply.

You don't need a revolutionary idea to think like an entrepreneur. You need the eyes to notice what everyone else overlooks—and the grit to design a solution that actually works.

Entrepreneurship is not about perfect business plans. It's about building the capacity to turn any problem into a system that delivers. Start with the annoyances you hear every day—the ones people keep grumbling about but never fix. That's where entrepreneurs are made.

Next up: we'll dive into how the teacher's instinct to develop others is one of the most underrated leadership superpowers you can stack.

CHAPTER 14
THE TEACHER'S TOOLKIT

The task of the modern educator is not to cut down jungles, but to irrigate deserts.

—*C. S. Lewis*

Caleb stood at the front of the classroom with a map of Europe rolled under his arm, dates neatly written on the board.

When he asked why the war had started, the students almost groaned. Some ventured a guess, but most of the room stayed silent. Painfully silent. One student asked to go to the bathroom.

That afternoon, alone in the classroom, Caleb sat at his desk and looked at his own notes on the board. It was a wall of abstract terms--*czar, duke, weltanschauung, deflation.* He realized something uncomfortable: these words didn't mean a thing to his students. In fact, reading them over, Caleb found himself yawning.

The next day, Caleb erased the board. He began with a story instead.

"Yesterday after school," he said, "Jimmy and Trisha argued in the hallway about a locker. Both said it belonged to them. Neither would back down."

Students giggled, but they tuned in.

"What made it turn into a fight?" Caleb asked.

"Pride."
"Everyone watching."
"They didn't want to look weak."

Caleb nodded. He drew a little rectangle on the board. Then another beside it.

"Now imagine the lockers are pieces of land," Caleb said, unrolling a map, "and the students have friends who promise to jump in if things go south."

He moved through Europe's history slowly, one country at a time, one event at a time. He stopped to ask questions to the class, to draw connections to their real experiences.

By Friday, the class was arguing about whether a leader had any good options left. They remembered dates because they remembered what had just gone wrong before them. Students started to stay after the bell, just to ask questions about what would happen next.

He learned to start with a story––*a why*. Students didn't care about "history," that assortment of dusty facts. They cared deeply about people and events related to *their* lives. And that made all the difference.

*
**

As Caleb discovered, knowledge without the ability to teach is just private knowledge. You may already hold skills or insights that could change people's lives—if only you knew how to transfer them. Teaching isn't just about expertise. Plenty of people have that in spades. It's about translation: turning difficult ideas into ones that *click*.

In this chapter, we'll break down the five core skills that transform book knowledge into useful lessons people love.

The Classroom That Changed Everything

As you know, I made the most of my time after COVID momentarily killed FlashPants in March 2020. I was in hotel conference rooms giving people a sneak peek into how the markets work and offering an opportunity to go deeper—not because I had always dreamed of being a teacher. Rather, I realized that there was a massive imbalance in the demand for market knowledge and the supply of effective teaching.

I'd spent years reading crowds for FlashPants. Now I was reading classrooms. The skill stack was largely the same, only the environment different. I'd often smile in amazement when I saw that the approaches I'd use on the stage were transferring to the classroom. The content, of course, was different—radically so. But what made a lesson compelling—and, importantly, what made it stick in the minds of my students—was surprisingly similar to what wowed an audience.

I'm one of the few people who teach these kinds of classes without talking much about myself. In fact, I'd bet I work harder than anyone else to keep myself out of a class. The less overly-technical jargon I shared, the more my class learned. That was the great paradox.

You don't teach by proving that you're the smartest person in the room. Rather, you do it by making everyone else smarter.

Teaching isn't a talent you're born with (or at least one I wasn't born with). Rather, the art of engaging teaching can be broken down into five smaller skills. We'll cover them now.

1. Knowledge Transfer: Translating What You Know into What They Can Do

Some people think that transferring know-how is like something out of *The Matrix*: uploading and downloading facts and data. Not so. It's about ordering ideas so people can build understanding step by step. In learning science, this is called *scaffolding*.

Knowledge transfer means:

- Start where they are, not where you are
- Break complex concepts into bite-sized chunks
- Relate new ideas to what they already know
- Check for comprehension before moving on

How I learned this:

When I lead trading workshops, I can't start with advanced strategies. I start with the basics: what a chart shows, the concept of price action, and only then move to more complex strategies. Each step has to land before I layer the next.

How it transfers:

- **Parenting:** Teach life skills from what kids already understand. ("Remember how you share toys? Money works the same way.")

- **Management:** Train employees by tying new tasks to processes they already know.

- **Relationships:** Explain your perspective using shared experiences instead of abstract logic.

2. Audience Analysis: Reading the Room in Real Time

You can tell in seconds whether someone's engaged or just nodding politely. We've all experienced it: you're telling a story to a group of friends, and one is nodding along while another hasn't reacted at all. You pause and ask, "Do you know what I mean?" and your friend admits he missed the beginning of the story.

Audience analysis means:

- Spotting confusion before they can articulate it

- Recognizing when someone's ready for the next level

- Noticing different learning styles within the same group

- Adjusting your strategy on the fly based on what you see

How I learned this:

When I lead trading workshops, every classroom has the same mix of learners, but they all absorb differently:

- **The Analyticals (logical-mathematical):** Engineers, accountants. They interrupt mid-sentence: "What's the win rate? Show me the backtest data." They need proof—numbers before action. Often, they need everything lined up with logical instructions: $A \rightarrow B \rightarrow C$. Skip a step and they are lost.

- **The Visuals (spatial):** They nod during explanations, but their eyes glaze over until I draw a chart or circle a trendline. Then they light up: "Oh, now I see it."

- **The Hands-On (kinesthetic):** Entrepreneurs, salespeople. They can't sit still through theory. "Can't we just trade already?" They need to push buttons, place orders, and make mistakes.

- **The Storytellers (verbal-linguistic):** They only understand once I turn it into a narrative. "The market panicked, ran for safety, then regained confidence."

Though the content and my teaching goal are often the same, I learned to use these four distinct delivery methods to enhance student retention.

How it transfers:

- **Team leadership:** Knowing who needs explicit, step-by-step directions versus broad, big-picture strategy.

- **Sales:** Spotting whether a prospect needs proof, story, or hands-on demo before they say yes.

- **Parenting:** Knowing when your kid needs encouragement versus when they need space to process.

3. Complex Simplification: Making Hard Things Easy

Complex simplification doesn't mean dumbing things down. It means taking the straightest route through complicated territory.

Complex simplification means:

- Using analogies that spark instant clarity

- Cutting jargon that only confuses

- Highlighting the 20% of concepts that drive 80% of results (Pareto principle)

- Making abstract ideas concrete and actionable

How I learned this:

Trading is full of intimidating terms. But if I said, "price action levels," most beginners froze. If instead I said, "think of them as turning points in price," people would relax.

How it transfers:

- **Management:** Translate corporate strategy into what employees do on Monday morning.

- **Health:** Explaining a diagnosis in everyday terms so patients know what's happening and what to do.

- **Technology:** Teaching new apps by comparing them to something people already use.

4. Motivation: Generating the Drive to Continue Learning

Motivation isn't pep talks. It's designing experiences where people feel capable and see progress.

Motivation means:

- Structuring quick wins that build confidence

- Showing visible progress even before mastery arrives

- Tying learning to personal goals so it feels meaningful

- Creating a safe environment where failure is part of the process

How I learned this:

Student traders needed early wins. I used simple practice exercises to get them placing basic trades right away, building confidence through action before moving into advanced concepts. Small, hands-on steps kept them far more engaged than explanations ever did.

How it transfers:

- **Fitness:** Small workouts that deliver results quickly while building long-term habits.

- **Parenting:** Celebrating small milestones to fuel kids' confidence for bigger challenges.

- **Team building:** Structuring projects so everyone contributes meaningfully from the start.

5. Results Tracking: Measuring What Truly Matters

Results tracking isn't about grading tests. It's about building feedback loops that show what's working, what's not, and where the adjustment needs to happen.

Results tracking means:

- Measuring application, not memorization

- Giving people safe environments to practice without real-world fallout

- Tracking progress toward practical outcomes, not abstract knowledge

- Treating mistakes as data, not as failures

How I learned this:

When I lead trading workshops, I don't focus on whether a student could recite technical definitions. What matters is whether they can apply concepts to make more informed decisions in realistic trading scenarios. Everything else, like flashcards and memorized rules, are just noise.

How it transfers:

- **Employee development:** Track whether people actually improve performance, not just whether they "completed the training."

- **Parenting:** Look for behavioral changes, not whether your kid can repeat back the rules.

- **Personal development:** Focus on habit formation and follow-through, not just setting aspirational goals.

The Why That Found Me

Here's the thing: I never set out to "find my purpose" as a teacher.

I didn't chase a calling. I stacked skills: reading people, simplifying concepts, creating systems. When the opportunity showed up, the stack was already there. When an opportunity to teach arose, my skills were ready.

That's how purpose works. You don't force it. You build skills. Skills open doors. Doors reveal purpose. And purpose creates impact. Most people think of this backwards.

Start with what you can do. Your *why* will follow.

The Teaching Moments Everywhere

When you cultivate these four skills, you realize something: everything is teaching.

- Every conversation is **knowledge transfer**
- Every meeting requires **audience analysis**
- Every explanation is an exercise in **complex simplification**
- Every relationship involves **motivation**
- Every interaction produces **trackable results**

Teaching isn't something you only do in classrooms. It's what you do anytime you want another human being to understand, apply, or grow from something you've shared.

Why Most "Smart" People Can't Teach

They think teaching is about proving how much they know. Wrong. Teaching is about transferring what you know into what someone else can do.

"Smart" teachers usually fail because:

- They skip steps that feel obvious to them
- They bury learners in jargon that feels "precise" but just confuses
- They rush because they're impatient with "basic" questions

But teaching isn't about you. It's about them. The second you make the shift, focusing on their progress instead of your expertise, you stop being a lecturer and start being a teacher.

Chapter 14 Activity: Your Teacher's Toolkit Evaluation

Time to audit your own ability to transfer knowledge, read the room, simplify complexity, motivate growth, and measure results. Teaching is not about what you know—it's about what others can do after interacting with you.

Step 1: Teaching Inventory

This Week's Scan:

- What do people always come to you for help with?

- What parts of your job could be delegated if you taught them?

- What life skills do you take for granted that others don't have?

- What mistakes have you made that others could avoid if you shared?

Knowledge Breakdown Test:

For each item, ask yourself:

- Can I break this down step by step?

- Do I know *why* each step matters?

- Can I explain it in plain, non-jargon language?

- Do I know the exact parts beginners usually get stuck on?

If you can't answer all four, you don't own that skill as a teacher yet—you just own it as a doer.

Step 2: Practice Simplification

This Week's Challenge:

Pick one complex topic you know well and explain it to a total beginner.

Examples:

- Explain your job to someone outside your field.

- Teach a hobby you've mastered to a complete novice.

- Share a life lesson with someone who's currently in the middle of that problem.

- Break down a system or process you use every day for someone who needs it.

Simplification Rules:

- No jargon, no insider language.
- Use analogies from everyday life.
- Stop every few sentences and check for comprehension.
- Focus on what they need to *do*, not how much you understand.

If they walk away confused, you failed—not them.

Step 3: Audience Assessment Practice

Real-Time Reading:

In three conversations this week, focus on whether they're *actually* getting it.

Watch for:

- Are their eyes locked in or glazing over?
- Are they asking clarifying questions or going silent?
- Do they bring it up later, proving it stuck?
- Can they explain it back in their own words?

Adjustment Practice:

- Pause the second you sense confusion.
- Speed up if they're clearly tracking.
- Swap in new examples if the first one bombs.
- Ask "What questions do you have?" instead of "Do you understand?"

Step 4: Results Tracking System

Design one simple feedback loop to measure whether your "teaching" is actually landing.

Examples:

- **Parenting:** Track a single behavior you're helping a child build (sharing, chores, self-control).
- **Management:** Track one specific skill you're coaching an employee on (communication, process ownership).
- **Mentoring:** Track one measurable goal you're guiding someone toward.
- **Personal:** Track your own progress in an area where you're both student

and teacher (fitness, a new skill, or a habit).

Tracking Criteria:

- Focus on **application, not recall.**

- Measure **behavior change, not knowledge.**

- Look for **patterns of improvement, not perfection.**

- Use the feedback to adjust your teaching style.

Teaching is a skill stack. By auditing, simplifying, reading, and tracking, you'll prove to yourself that you don't need a classroom or title to be a teacher, you just need the discipline to make others more capable because of you. Scan to access the Teaching Template:

Wrapping It Up

I didn't become a financial educator because I set out to teach. It happened as skills like reading people, simplifying complexity, motivating effort, and tracking progress were put to use in a new setting—much like when I taught drumming lessons years earlier.

Your abilities as a teacher show up in every conversation, every relationship, every moment where you help someone make sense of something new. The real issue isn't whether you *know enough* to teach. The real issue is whether you can put their learning ahead of your ego.

You already hold knowledge that could transform someone's life. The question is whether you'll build the skill to deliver it in a way that lands. Start small—one person, one concept, one conversation where you focus entirely on *their* understanding instead of proving *your* expertise. That's how real teachers are made.

Now that we've covered how to transfer knowledge, it's time to explore the **Connector's Code**—the invisible skill that determines whether you're building a network of real allies or just collecting names in your phone.

CHAPTER 15
THE CONNECTOR'S CODE

It is not so much our friends' help that helps us, as the confidence of their help.

—Epicurus

Joel had been "networking" for three years. Industry conferences. LinkedIn ads. Stacks of business cards. His database boasted 847 contacts. But when his startup needed capital, he couldn't think of a single person to call.

"I don't get it," he told his co-worker, Elizabeth. "I know everyone in this industry. Every mixer, every happy hour—I was there."

Elizabeth scrolled through his contact list. "How many of these people would take your call on a Sunday? How many know what you're really building? How many have you helped with something that mattered to them?"

Joel had no answer.

"You've been collecting contacts," Elizabeth said. "Not building relationships. There's a difference."

"So what do I do?" Joel asked.

"Pick ten people on this list," Elizabeth said. "Not the fanciest titles—the ones you actually enjoyed talking to. Spend the next month adding value to *their* lives instead of asking for anything."

"Adding value… how?"

"Simple. Introduce them to someone they should know. Share an article that matters to their business. Follow up on something they told you. Show you were listening."

Joel hesitated. "But won't that feel random? Some of these people I haven't spoken to in months."

"That's exactly why it works. Most people only reach out when they want something. If you reach out to *give* something, you immediately stand out."

So Joel did it. Ten people. One month. He reconnected without an agenda. He made introductions, sent insights, and supported projects. By the time he needed funding, three of the ten either invested or connected him to investors.

Six months later, Joel's startup was funded—not from names in a database, but from just eight genuine relationships he'd built.

"The biggest leap," Joel admitted, "wasn't meeting more people. It was actually getting to know the people I already knew."

*
**

As Joel discovered, networking without relationships is just structured small talk. You may be mistaking visibility for connection. In this chapter, we'll break down the five essential skills that turn strangers into allies and contacts into community.

The Weekend That Changed Everything

I'd been a member of a global men's group for years, but I was a ghost. I lurked on the forums. One day, a moderator from the community, Moff, organized an in-person weekend in San Diego: Three days of brotherhood—storytelling, shared meals, and a Navy SEAL-style bootcamp on the very beaches where SEALs train.

I signed up instantly. Not because I knew what to expect. Because my gut told me this mattered. The first morning, at 4:00 AM, we stood along the cold shore in Coronado Beach. The sun had no hint at rising.

Within minutes, we were thrown into the freezing Pacific by Navy SEALs. Then we crawled ashore for burpees in the surf. Our lungs burned. Before we could catch our breath, came buddy carries through the waves, followed by push-ups in the sand. We were aching, frozen silhouettes on the shore. Then we were called back into the ocean. I tasted the saltwater. I felt it in my lungs as I gasped while waves slammed into us.

Halfway through, I needed oxygen. (Later, a medic confirmed that I actually needed oxygen.)

But I didn't quit. I pushed until my body had nothing left to give.

Here's what I wrote to the group afterward, unedited:

I've been a member of our community almost since its inception, but I rarely engaged in our online forums because I felt I didn't have much to contribute. I also had never attended any meetups until this past weekend in San Diego.

When Moff organized the event, I signed up immediately, intrigued by the chance to meet him and others from the community since I live in Southern California. I was immensely impressed by how well Moff managed the entire weekend. Planning an event for a dozen men is a challenging task, but he excelled—ensuring we had a fully stocked fridge, facilitating sharing our origin stories, shared meals, and organizing unforgettable bonding experiences, while striking the perfect balance of allowing enough free time for us to do our own things.

By Sunday, I had transformed from a stranger to feeling part of a brotherhood I never imagined I could belong to. I'm now looking forward to more meetups, not just for the camaraderie but also for the genuine connections and potential business partnerships that emerge.

The weekend included an incredible challenge: being trained by Navy SEALs on Coronado Beach, which is where actual Navy SEALs train. Despite not being the strongest, fastest, or youngest, I pushed myself to the limits. This effort earned me respect from the group, reinforcing that true brotherhood doesn't hinge on being the best—it's about showing heart and commitment. This experience taught me that respect and trust can grow quickly among those who are willing to give their all.

Truly inspiring to be part of a diverse community of men up to big things, who are willing to DO THE WORK!

What that experience taught me was that brotherhood, community, and unity are forged by difficulty. And that's when the unexpected hit me.

The guys who were stronger, faster, tougher—they didn't judge me for struggling. They respected me for my heart. That's when I understood that brotherhood depends on showing up for your people, whether you're having your best day or your worst.

Skills That Create True Connection

That weekend I discovered something most people never learn: connection is not networking. Connection is built on five specific skills that apply everywhere—whether you're cultivating business relationships, deepening family ties, or forging lifelong friendships.

1. Building Relationships: Forming Lasting Bonds

Relationship building isn't about what you can *get* from people. It's about what you *give.*

Relationship building means:

- Leading with value, not need
- Remembering what matters to them, not just what they do
- Showing up consistently, not just when you need something
- Investing in people long before you know how they might benefit you

How I learned this:

On that beach, nobody cared about titles or bank accounts. We cared about who had your back when you were gasping for breath. Authentic relationships are forged when people see you at your most vulnerable.

How it transfers:

- *Business:* Partnerships built on reciprocity, not transactions
- *Marriage:* Connection through shared challenge and support
- *Parenting:* Trust built by consistency, not control

2. Building Trust: Achieving Credibility Through Vulnerability

Trust doesn't come from perfection. It comes from being real.

Trust creation means:

- Sharing struggles, not just successes
- Admitting what you don't know instead of faking expertise
- Following through on small commitments to earn confidence in big ones
- Being the same person in private as you are in public

How I learned this:

When I struggled on that beach, I could've acted fine. Instead, I let them see me fight through it. That vulnerability built trust faster than any résumé ever could. And that night, during the *origin story circle,* a dozen men shared their life journeys—raw, unfiltered. Each story ended with feedback from the group and suggestions for change. That vulnerability cracked us open. Trust cemented instantly.

How it transfers:

- *Leadership:* Teams trust leaders who own mistakes and doubts
- *Sales:* Clients trust honesty more than polished perfection
- *Friendship:* Bonds deepen when you share what's really happening in your life

3. Community Development: Creating Spaces Where Individuals Thrive

Community development isn't about being the star of the show. It's about building a stage where *everyone* gets to shine.

Community development means:

- Facilitating connections between others, not just connecting people to yourself
- Designing shared experiences that unify rather than isolate
- Recognizing and celebrating people's strengths and contributions
- Creating a culture where people feel *ownership*, not just membership

How I learned this:

Moff didn't just plan logistics that weekend. He built a container where every man's contribution mattered. Someone stocked the fridge. Someone cooked meals. Someone told stories that broke open conversations. The event worked because it wasn't about one leader—it was about *all of us stepping up.*

How it transfers:

- *Team building:* Creating workplace culture where every voice has weight
- *Family:* Building homes where each person contributes their unique strength
- *Social groups:* Hosting events that draw out the best in everyone instead of centering on one ego

4. Vulnerability: Strength Through Authenticity

Vulnerability isn't weakness. It's courage under a spotlight.

Vulnerability means:

- Sharing struggles without turning them into pity parties
- Asking for help without apologizing for needing it
- Expressing emotions without losing control
- Being honest about weaknesses while working to improve them

How I learned this:

After that weekend, I wrote my testimonial: "Despite not being the strongest, fastest, or youngest, I pushed myself to the limits. This effort earned me respect from the group." I didn't earn trust by dominating. I earned it by showing heart.

How it transfers:

- *Marriage:* Intimacy grows when you share fears and needs openly
- *Management:* Teams rally when you admit challenges and invite solutions
- *Friendship:* Real bonds form when you let others see what's behind the mask

5. Leadership: Leading Without Dictating

Leadership isn't about control. It's about creating conditions where solutions emerge.

Leadership is:

- Setting standards through behavior, not rules
- Developing others instead of showcasing yourself
- Taking responsibility when things go wrong and giving credit when they go right
- Building safety so others feel free to risk, experiment, and grow

How I learned this:

The men I respected most that weekend weren't barking orders. They were the ones who stayed calm under pressure, pulled you forward when you were fading, and modeled what they asked of others.

How it transfers:

- *Business:* Inspiring teams through influence and example, not command and control
- *Parenting:* Guiding kids by modeling behaviors you want them to adopt

- *Community:* Sparking collective action through service and example

The Transformation

By Sunday, I had gone from a stranger to feeling part of a brotherhood I never imagined I'd belong to.

Not because I impressed anyone.

But because I showed up authentically—and let them watch me struggle.

That's the connector's code: people don't connect to your achievements. They connect to your *struggles.*

Why Most Networking Fails

Most people keep score with the wrong scoreboard.

- They count contacts instead of connections.
- They optimize reach instead of depth.
- They start with what they want instead of what they can give.

That's why so many professionals "know everyone" but can't call anyone when it matters. Real connection happens when you stop trying to be impressive and start trying to be useful.

The strongest networks aren't transactional. They're transformational. They're built in moments where you help someone become a better version of themselves— and they never forget it.

The Brotherhood Multiplier

Here's the paradox: the more you focus on yourself, the less people want to follow you. The more you focus on others, the more magnetic you become.

When you link people to each other, add value to the group, and prioritize their success over your own spotlight, something counterintuitive happens: you become the hub.

Not because you claimed it. Because you *earned it through service.*

Chapter 15 Activity: Your Connector's Code Evaluation

Time to stop collecting contacts and start stacking real connections. Use this four-step evaluation to audit your inner circle, practice vulnerability, develop community, and systematize your relationship building.

Step 1: Brotherhood/Sisterhood Audit

Your Current Inner Circle:

- Who are the 5 people you'd call in a crisis?

- Who would actually drop everything to show up?

- Whose hardest battles have you walked through with them?

- With whom are you your *real* self—not just your highlight reel?

Relationship Quality Check:

For each key relationship, ask yourself:

- When was the last time you added value without being asked?

- What are they chasing that you could help accelerate?

- Do they share their *real* struggles with you, or just surface-level chatter?

- How has this relationship forced you to grow?

Step 2: Practicing Vulnerability

This Week's Challenge:

Pick one relationship and practice *strategic vulnerability.*

Examples:

- Share a current struggle (without fishing for advice).

- Admit something you don't know but want to learn.

- Ask for help on something you usually do solo.

- Express direct gratitude for their influence on your life.

Guidelines:

- Share struggle, not just highlight reels.

- Be truthful, not dramatic.

- Ask for help, not pity.

- Frame it as growth, not as a problem dump.

Step 3: Community Development Opportunity

Ask yourself: Where could I create value for more than one person at once?

Possibilities:

- Run a skill-sharing session at work.
- Host a small gathering that connects people in your industry.
- Start a support group for people tackling the same challenge.
- Facilitate introductions between people who should meet.

Action Principles:

- Spotlight others' wins, not your own.
- Build shared experiences that outlast the moment.
- Give credit often and loudly.
- Create something that doesn't depend on you every day.

Step 4: Relationship Building System

Platform & Procedure:

Pick your lane—text, LinkedIn, phone calls, dinners. Then build a repeatable system.

Weekly Habits:

- Reach out to 3 people just to check in—no agenda.
- Share one useful resource.
- Make one warm intro between two people.
- Follow up on a past conversation.

Monthly Practices:

- Host one small event (virtual or in-person).
- Publicly celebrate someone else's success.
- Ask one person directly: "How can I help you right now?"
- Review which relationships need more energy.

Quarterly Reviews:

- Audit: Which relationships are deepening vs. staying surface?

- Reconnect with someone you lost touch with but care about.

- Plan one meaningful shared experience with your core circle.

- Adjust your system based on what's creating the deepest bonds.

Pro tip: Your system doesn't need to be complicated. Consistency beats complexity every time. Show up weekly, invest monthly, and design quarterly. That's how you stack trust that compounds for life.

Wrapping It Up

That weekend in San Diego didn't just teach me the meaning of brotherhood—it showed me the mechanics of authentic connection. Real trust requires that you bring all of yourself: your strengths, your weaknesses, and your willingness to walk with others through theirs.

The men who earned respect weren't the ones with the best résumés. They were the ones who tried, who risked vulnerability, who served the group. Respect came from effort, not ego. Connection came from contribution, not credentials.

Your network isn't your contact list. It's the handful of people who know the real you and still choose to invest in your forward motion.

Build that network one real conversation at a time. Lead with what you can give, not what you want to get. Show up when it's inconvenient, not just when it's easy. That's how communities form, and that's how they endure.

Now that we've broken down the code of building real relationships, it's time to explore how a different kind of skill—the healer's ability to create distinct value—becomes a competitive advantage in any market.

CHAPTER 16
THE HEALER'S HEART

Act as if what you do makes a difference. It does.

—William James

Susanna had been running her marketing business for five years. Steady profits. Loyal clients. Comfortable lifestyle. On paper, she had everything most freelancers dream of. But something was missing.

"I just keep feeling like there has to be more to it," she confessed to her therapist, Dr. Chen. "I'm making a living, but I'm not making a difference. I look at world issues—poverty, education, food security—and I feel powerless."

Dr. Chen leaned in. "What would 'making a difference' look like to you?"

"I don't know. Something big. Ending poverty. Solving world hunger. Something that matters."

"What if the impact wasn't about the size of the problem, but the depth of the change you create for specific people?"

Susanna frowned. "But what can one person actually do?"

Dr. Chen told her the story of two burned-out Americans on vacation. They met Mia, a woman whose family's small sari-sari store had been shuttered for years. The whole village relied on it for basics—soap, rice, cold drinks—but the family couldn't afford to reopen.

Over dinner, the men realized their vacation budget could do more than buy cocktails. At 55 pesos to the dollar, a few thousand bucks could transform a community. They partnered with Mia's uncle to refurbish the shop, restock inventory, and get the doors open. Within a month, the bright green hut was humming again. Kids bought candy. Parents grabbed necessities. Profits even funded lunches at the local church.

"They didn't end world hunger," Dr. Chen said. "But they ended one family's hunger. And the ripple spread further than they imagined."

Susanna was quiet. "But I'm not traveling to far-off islands."

"You don't have to. Start with what you already do well. Where are your skills most desperately needed but least available?"

Susanna thought about it. "Marketing. Web design. Helping businesses get found online."

"Exactly. Now think about nonprofits, schools, or community groups with great missions but terrible marketing. They don't need another volunteer. They need visibility. They need you."

Two weeks later, Susanna discovered a nonprofit school in Guatemala trying to fund a computer lab. Their website looked like it was built in 1995, their social media was nonexistent, and their fundraising materials were ineffective. She offered to rebuild their entire online presence pro bono.

Six months later, the school had a professional website, compelling stories, email campaigns, and an active social presence. The result? $23,400 raised—enough to build the lab and provide scholarships for twelve students.

"I realized," Susanna later said, "impact isn't about chasing bigger problems. It's about strategically applying what you already know in places that desperately need it."

*
**

Just as Susanna learned that meaningful impact doesn't always mean changing careers or solving world hunger, you might be underestimating how your current skills and resources could change lives right now. The leverage isn't in waiting for the perfect moment or the perfect cause. It's in stacking what you already do well with where it's most needed.

This chapter will show you the five essential skills that turn good intentions into measurable impact, whether in business, community, or personal life:

The Vacation That Became a Mission

In 2024, Graysen and I were exhausted. FlashPants, trading, teaching—just two workaholics grinding nonstop. Taking a vacation felt like admitting we were slacking. If we weren't building, we were lazy. But Graysen had vacation days piling up, and I carved out a window. So, we said, "Screw it, let's hit the Philippines for three weeks." No laptops, no deals—just food, island-hopping, snorkeling in crystal waters so blue they looked fake. It was supposed to be a reset, a chance to breathe.

Three days in, I was crawling out of my skin. Lounging on a beach felt wrong when I could be closing a deal or tweaking a system. Graysen was just as bad, sneaking phone checks, itching for a project. We weren't wired for idleness. But that restlessness, that workaholic itch, led us to something bigger than a tan. It led us to what I now call "micro-philanthropy"—small acts that punch way above their weight.

A Sari-Sari Store and a Spark

On a tiny island, we met Mia, a woman whose family owned a patch of land with a sari-sari store—a little hut, the village's Quick Mart, stocked with snacks, soap, drinks, whatever locals needed. She told us it used to be the heart of the community, a bustling hub, but it had been shuttered for years, dilapidated and forgotten. Her family couldn't afford the restart. Mia's voice carried pride but also a quiet defeat, like a dream left to rot.

Graysen and I locked eyes. We'd always looked for ways to give back when traveling, and here was a chance. The dollar stretched far—55 pesos to the dollar—and we saw an opening to make a real dent. Over a plate of adobo, we pitched Mia an idea: we'd donate seed capital to revive the store. She brought in her uncle, William, a family man with a sharp business mind. On a crackly Zoom call, we mapped it out: clean the hut, slap on fresh paint, stock it with chips, soda, soap, rice. We'd fund it, they'd run it. No strings, just impact.

Micro-Philanthropy in Action

It took a month. We wired the money—enough to refurbish, restock, and relaunch. Mia sent photos: a bright green hut, shelves bursting with goods, a hand-painted sign glowing at dusk. The store reopened, and the village showed up. Kids grabbed candies, moms bought rice, guys snagged beers. It was alive again, a heartbeat restored. William's emails were gold: "We're feeding kids at the church now, thanks to you." One photo showed a dozen smiling children, plates piled with food, because the store's profits fueled community meals.

That's micro-philanthropy: small, leveraged acts that transform lives. With 55 pesos to a dollar, a few thousand bucks rebuilt a village's lifeline. We've never taken a dime back. Instead, we coach them—sales tips, inventory hacks, marketing ideas. William's progress reports are humbling: "More customers every week, thank you for believing in us." A call last month had him grinning, sharing how they added a new soda cooler, doubling drink sales. What distinguishes micro-philanthropy is its ability to unlock potential and create pathways where none existed before. I even made a website for them—MSGSariSari.com.

The Butterfly Effect of Self-Care

But here's what really matters: take away that vacation with Graysen, and this entire scenario crumbles. We're selfish workaholics—always grinding, rarely resting. Downtime felt like failure, like we were letting the hustle down. But what we realized is that skipping self-care doesn't just screw you—it screws the world. If we hadn't gone to the Philippines, we'd never have met Mia, never revived that store, never fed those kids. Our burnout would've blocked a butterfly effect that rippled across an ocean.

Self-care isn't selfish; it's a prerequisite for stacking humanity. As workaholics, we had to learn that recharging isn't slacking—it's fuel for impact. That three-week trip, snorkeling and eating our weight in lumpia, gave us the clarity to see Mia's need and act. If you're grinding yourself into the ground, you're not just hurting you—you're robbing the world of the possibilities you could create. Take the damn vacation. Step away. The butterfly effect might just transform lives you'd never imagine, like a village store lighting up a community.

The Five Skills That Bring Lasting Change

That experience taught me that meaningful impact isn't about the size of your gesture. It's about mastering five specific skills that turn resources into results:

1. Impact Creation: Finding Leverage Points That Matter

Creating impact is not about tackling the biggest global issues. It's about spotting modest interventions that create disproportionate outcomes.

Impact creation means:

- Looking for high-leverage, low-cost solutions
- Prioritizing sustainable change over short-term relief
- Addressing root causes instead of surface symptoms
- Measuring outcomes, not just outputs

How I learned this:

We didn't try to "end Philippine poverty." We found one family with one solvable problem. A few thousand dollars reopened a village store that became the community's economic lifeline.

How it transfers:

- *Business:* Build employee programs that improve retention more than salary bumps.
- *Community:* Create neighborhood solutions that prevent problems before they start.
- *Family:* Build systems that stop recurring stress instead of constantly firefighting it.

2. Resource Leveraging: Maximizing What You Already Have

Resource leveraging isn't about throwing money at problems. It's about squeezing maximum value out of what you already possess.

Resource leveraging means:

- Valuing skills and relationships as much as cash
- Finding opportunities where your dollar stretches furthest
- Stacking multiple resource types for multiplied effect
- Timing interventions for maximum efficiency

How I learned this:

The exchange rate meant our vacation money went far. But we didn't just write a check. We added business coaching on sales, inventory, and marketing. Money plus knowledge created exponential results.

How it transfers:

- *Career:* Use your network and expertise to open doors for others (and yourself).
- *Parenting:* Leverage your knowledge and connections to expand opportunities for your kids.
- *Community service:* Donate skills that carry more value than money alone.

3. Cultural Sensitivity: Building Change That Honors Context

As we offered our services, assistance, and money, we made sure to honor the cultural context we were operating on.

Cultural sensitivity means:

- Gathering local knowledge before suggesting fixes
- Partnering with community leaders rather than bypassing them
- Respecting existing relationships and hierarchies
- Aligning with cultural patterns instead of imposing foreign ones

How I learned this:

We didn't impose an American business model. We worked through Mia and William, who already knew the local dynamics. They ran the store their way. We provided resources and advice without stepping imposing our cultural opinions. We even met with the Mayor of Lapu-Lapu City, in part to show respect.

How it transfers:

- *Management:* Implement change in alignment with team culture.
- *Marriage:* Build solutions that respect both partners' styles.
- *Neighborhood:* Launch projects through trusted relationships, not around them.

4. Sustainable Giving: Creating Systems That Last Without You

Sustainable giving isn't charity. It's building systems that keep producing after you step away.

Sustainable giving means:

- Building capacity, not dependency
- Teaching skills, not just supplying resources
- Generating revenue streams, not just offsetting costs
- Creating systems that improve over time

How I learned this:

We didn't commit to monthly donations. We invested in a business. The store earns its own revenue, and part of that revenue funds meals for kids at the local church. That's sustained impact from a one-time investment.

How it transfers:

- *Employee development:* Train skills that transfer anywhere, not just inside your company.

- *Mentoring:* Teach frameworks that create ongoing growth instead of fixing one problem at a time.

- *Family:* Develop your kids' independence rather than setting up permanent reliance.

5. Global Thinking: Looking Beyond Your Immediate Circle

Global thinking isn't about solving world problems. It's recognizing that your smallest actions can ripple further than you'll ever see.

Global thinking means:

- Seeing how small actions create outsized consequences

- Hunting for opportunities where few others are looking

- Recognizing different markets hold different leverage points

- Bridging your world with worlds you normally wouldn't touch

How I learned this:

That trip to the Philippines was supposed to be a vacation. Instead, it turned into a chain reaction: vacation led us to Mia's store, which led us to building up a community. Kids today are fed by the economic impact we were able to make in that city. One butterfly effect stretched across an ocean.

How it transfers:

- *Business networking:* Build relationships in markets others ignore.

- *Skill development:* Learn capabilities that set you apart in overlooked spaces.

- *Investing:* Place capital where few are paying attention, but upside is massive.

These five skills—Impact Creation, Resource Leveraging, Cultural Sensitivity,

Sustainable Giving, and Global Thinking—are the levers that turn good intentions into lasting, measurable change.

Micro-Philanthropy vs. Macro Guilt

Most people look at global problems (poverty, war, famine) and freeze. "What can I possibly do?" Wrong question. The right question is: *What specific problem can I solve for specific people with the resources I have today?*

Micro-philanthropy isn't "small." It's surgical. It focuses resources where they matter most. A $200 check to a bloated charity gets absorbed. That same $200, targeted at the right leverage point, can change lives.

Why Most Charitable Giving Fails

Because it's lazy. People write checks to feel good instead of solving problems. They donate to symptoms instead of systems.

Real impact requires the same five entrepreneurial muscles we've been building all along:

- Spot the real problem.
- Design a solution that works.
- Leverage resources wisely.
- Build systems that last.
- Scale through ripple effects.

The difference between charity and impact is the difference between a band-aid and a cure.

Chapter 16 Activity: Your Healer's Heart Inventory

Time to evaluate your impact-creation skills and start stacking your abilities into measurable change.

Step 1: Micro-Philanthropy Opportunity Scan

Your Current Assets:

- What skills do you have that others urgently need?
- What financial resources could you deploy strategically instead of reactively?

- What networks or connections could open doors for others?
- What knowledge or experience could you share to shortcut someone else's struggle?

Problem Identification:

- What issues do you see again and again in your community?
- Where is inefficiency or waste crying out for a better system?
- What needs are people expressing that aren't being met effectively?
- Where could a small intervention create disproportionate results?

Leverage Assessment:

- Where would your skills, time, or money stretch the furthest?
- Which problems align with your strengths?
- Where is nobody else competing for the opportunity?
- What would create long-term value beyond your direct participation?

Step 2: Resource Leveraging Practice

This Month's Experiment: Choose one method to put your resources to work:

Skill Leveraging:

- Provide pro bono services in your field to a nonprofit.
- Teach someone a skill you've mastered.
- Lend your professional expertise to a community project.

Network Leveraging:

- Introduce two people who should know each other.
- Connect someone to an opportunity they couldn't reach alone.
- Use your network to solve a problem for someone without one.

Knowledge Leveraging:

- Share information that improves someone's decision-making.
- Mentor a person through a challenge you've already faced.
- Create content that helps others avoid the mistakes you made.

Step 3: Planning for Impact Creation

Problem Selection:

- Choose a specific issue affecting specific people.

- Focus on what you can realistically influence.

- Pick something you can measure with clear outcomes.

- Align the opportunity with your available resources.

Solution Design:

- Begin with the result you want to create.

- Work backwards to the simplest effective intervention.

- Design for sustainability, not just short-term relief.

- Build in measurement and feedback loops.

Implementation Strategy:

- Set a clear timeline and budget.

- Identify local partners who know the context.

- Establish accountability for follow-through.

- Plan for long-term engagement, not just a one-off gesture.

Step 4: Balancing Service and Self-Care

Evaluate Your Current Balance:

- Are you helping so much that you're burning yourself out?

- Are you protecting your self-care so much that you're making no outside impact?

- Where would better self-care actually make you more effective in serving others?

- Which self-care practices would fuel—not just restore—your capacity to give?

Integration Plan:

- Design self-care that recharges you for service, not just survival.

- Schedule service in alignment with your values so it renews your purpose.

- Set boundaries that protect your ability for long-term impact.

- Create rhythms that support both growth and contribution.

The healer's heart isn't about overextending yourself. It's about creating targeted impact while staying grounded enough to keep showing up for the long haul.

Wrapping It Up

That sari-sari store is still running. William sends photos and videos: more customers each week, steady profits, community meals funded, children fed—all because two burned-out workaholics finally took a break. He's even started a successful seashell business. We didn't need a master plan to change the world. We just needed to notice an opportunity and apply our skills with intention.

Your influence isn't limited by the size of your bank account. It's limited by the scope of your thinking and the strategic use of what you already have. Start with one specific issue you can address for real people using the resources at your disposal today.

That's how healing happens, one strategic intervention at a time.

CHAPTER 17
THE HEALTH-WEALTH STACK

The greatest wealth is health.

—Virgil

Abel had spent eight years building a thriving consulting practice. Six-figure income. Blue-chip clients. Admired expertise. On paper, he was winning. Inside, he was falling apart.

"I'm earning more than ever," he admitted to his doctor, "but I feel awful. I'm wiped out by 2 PM, stressed all the time, and I can't even focus on client calls."

Dr. Roberts scanned the lab results. "Your cortisol is sky-high. Blood pressure's up. You're pre-diabetic. When's the last time you exercised?"

Abel shrugged. "I don't have time. I'm building a business."

Dr. Roberts leaned forward. "You're not building a business. You're depleting the one resource that makes it possible—your health. Let me ask you this: how much is that post-lunch brain haze costing you in lost deals?"

Abel froze. Just last month he had botched two afternoon calls because he couldn't think straight. Both prospects walked.

"Start here," Dr. Roberts said. "Swap your big lunches with smaller ones. Instead of digesting a heavy meal, your body will feel lighter and your mind will be sharper. More clarity, more energy—and ironically, more time in your day."

Skeptical but desperate, Abel tried it. The very first week, his 3 PM call was sharp. He landed a $50,000 project he'd been chasing for months. Hungry for more advice, Abel came back to Dr. Roberts's office the following week.

"Interesting," he told Dr. Roberts. "What else?"

"Exercise. Twenty minutes of resistance training, twice a week. Push-ups, squats, lunges—whatever you can do. Physical strength equals mental presence. You'll negotiate differently when you feel strong."

Abel added quick office workouts between calls. Within weeks, he noticed he no longer avoided tough client conversations.

Next came meditation to prepare his mind for high-stakes calls, and sauna sessions he first dismissed as indulgence—until he realized he was sleeping better and thinking sharper the next morning.

Six months later, Abel's bloodwork was normal, his stress was lower, and his business was up 40%.

"The breakthrough," he told Dr. Roberts, "wasn't choosing between health and wealth. It was realizing they're the same system."

*
**

As Abel discovered, health and wealth aren't competing priorities—they're two sides of the same stack. You may think you're juggling opposites, but in reality they're just different expressions of the same underlying habits. This chapter will teach you how to layer health and wealth so they reinforce each other instead of fighting for your time and attention.

The Protocol That Changed Everything

I'm not a health professional. I'm not a biohacker. I'm someone who realized that if I wanted to stack skills, wealth, and impact for the long haul, I had to stack health skills too. The practices in this chapter reflect my personal experience; consult a qualified professional before making significant changes to your health routine.

Still, I didn't build my system out of obsession with optimization. I built it out of obsession with sustainability. I won't suggest eliminating salt forever or enduring endless hours on the treadmill. Rather, my practices are battle-born: a skill stack that keeps me sharp, calm, and resilient without being needlessly burdened.

Healthy, Wealthy is Wise

Most people get health and wealth backwards. They think healthy habits pull time and focus away from wealth creation. These people grind away to eke out dollars from long work hours, high-pressure environments, and time away from family and friends.

Let me be clear: this is dead wrong.

The right health habits *create* the energy, focus, and endurance that make wealth possible. My health stack isn't separate from business—it's the cornerstone of it.

Meditation

What I do: Sit quietly for 5–15 minutes most mornings. No incense, no chanting—just space between my thoughts and actions.

- **Health benefit:** Lowers cortisol, steadies emotions, improves concentration
- **Wealth benefit:** Sharper decision-making, better negotiations, fewer stress-driven mistakes

Example: Before leading a 3-day trading intensive, meditation keeps me calm enough to manage 50+ students. Without it, I'd be reactive instead of responsive.

Resistance Training

What I do: Two lifting sessions a week. Sometimes three. Simple compound lifts—nothing fancy.

- **Health benefit:** Functional strength, stronger bones, better metabolism
- **Wealth benefit:** Physical strength fuels professional confidence, discipline bleeds into business habits

Example: Grinding out a tough set under the bar is the same mental toughness I use grinding out hard client conversations. Same muscle, different application.

Walking

What I do: Aim for 10,000 steps a day. About 90 minutes, spread throughout the day.

- **Health benefit:** Better heart health, lower stress, faster recovery
- **Wealth benefit:** Walking meetings spark creativity, problem-solving clicks into place while moving, relationships grow during shared walks

Example: My best business ideas never come at a desk. They come while I'm moving. My body unlocks my mind.

Intermittent Fasting

What I do: During 3-day classes, I usually fast most of the day—just lemon water and electrolytes.

- **Health benefit:** Greater metabolic flexibility, sharper mental clarity, reduced inflammation

- **Wealth benefit:** No energy crashes, laser focus through long workdays, no food decision fatigue

Example: I can teach for 8 hours straight while fasting and stay mentally sharp. Fasting keeps my energy steady instead of crashing from meals.

Sauna

What I do: 3–4 times a week, 15–20 minutes. Sweat, breathe, reset.

- **Health benefit:** Better heart health, reduced stress, faster recovery
- **Wealth benefit:** Manages burnout, deeper sleep for sharper next-day performance, recovery that lets me sustain higher intensity work

Example: After heavy teaching or travel, the sauna resets my system so I bounce back faster and keep operating at the top of my game.

The point isn't to do *my* exact routine. The point is to design a **stack of habits** that makes you sharper at both health and wealth, because they're the same game.

The Wealth Stack That Generates Health Freedom

Here's the flip side: the right wealth-creation habits give you the freedom and resources to invest in health.

Systems Thinking

What it is: Building systems that run without your constant presence.

- **Wealth benefit:** Passive income, scalable models, reclaimed time.
- **Health benefit:** Lower stress, more time for healthy routines, mental bandwidth for self-care.

Example: FlashPants runs on systems. I can step into a sauna or a gym session without business grinding to a halt.

Long-Term Investing

What it is: Building wealth through compound growth, not shortcuts.

- **Wealth benefit:** Financial freedom, asset growth, less money stress.
- **Health benefit:** A compound mindset—patience, sustainability, no crash-and-burn approaches.

Example: Understanding compound returns taught me to see workouts the same way. One session doesn't matter. Stacked over years, it's unstoppable.

Risk Management

What it is: Protecting the downside instead of betting it all on one thing.

- **Wealth benefit:** Diversified income, long-term growth, fewer wipeouts.
- **Health benefit:** A balanced routine that prevents injury, burnout, or all-or-nothing failure.

Example: Just like I don't bet everything on one investment, I don't leave my health to a single habit. When I have time for 10,000 steps and a long trip to the sauna, I do them. When I don't, I find alternatives (like calisthenics) that still confer health benefits.

Value Creation

What it is: Generating wealth by solving real problems for real people.

- **Wealth benefit:** Sustainable earnings, market credibility, purpose-driven growth.
- **Health benefit:** Meaningful work reduces stress, purpose fuels energy, service keeps you mentally strong.

Example: My businesses make money *because* they help others. That alignment lowers stress and creates fulfillment that's as healthy as any supplement.

The Compound Effect

Here's where it gets powerful: the stacks reinforce each other.

Meditation sharpens trading decisions → which reduces financial stress → which improves sleep → which boosts workout performance → which builds confidence → which fuels bigger business risks.

They're not separate. They're an integrated system. Each habit multiplies the others.

The Energy ROI Framework

I measure health investments the same way I measure financial ones: return on energy.

High ROI Health Habits

- Meditation: 15 minutes → 8 hours of sharper focus
- Resistance training: 1 hour → 24 hours of increased confidence and anti-aging benefits (like preventing muscle loss)
- Walking: 90 minutes → creativity unlocked, stress reduced
- Fasting: 0 minutes → mental clarity and stable energy regained

Low ROI Health Habits

- Social Media
- Overcomplicated supplement stacks with no clear payoff
- Extreme diets that create stress and aren't sustainable
- Workouts so intense they cause injury or burnout
- Routines that only work under "perfect" conditions

The goal isn't to do everything. It's to focus on the practices that deliver the **highest energy ROI** for the **lowest time investment.**

That's the health-wealth stack: a closed-loop system where each side funds and strengthens the other.

Why Most People Fail at Both

They frame health and wealth as enemies instead of allies.

They say: "I don't have time for the gym—I have to work." The truth: "The gym gives me the energy to work better."

They think: "I can't afford healthy food—I need to save money." The truth: "Healthy food is an investment in the focus that produces wealth."

They chase short-term productivity instead of long-term sustainability. And it costs them both.

The Integration Mindset

When you realize health and wealth are the same system, everything shifts:

- Morning rituals become business preparation, not time away from business

- Exercise becomes confidence training, not just physical maintenance

- Nutrition becomes cognitive enhancement, not just weight control

- Sleep becomes performance optimization, not just rest

- Stress management becomes decision-making improvement, not just relaxation

Every health habit fuels wealth creation. Every wealth habit creates health freedom.[2]

Health and wealth aren't separate paths. They're a single integrated stack. Get them working together, and you multiply both. Scan this code for the Energy ROI Calculator:

Chapter 17 Activity: Your Health-Wealth Stack Assessment

Time to consolidate your health and wealth creation into one integrated system.

Step 1: Current Integration Audit

Health Habits Analysis

- Which habits consistently boost your work energy?

- Which habits *feel* like they steal productivity time?

- Where is poor health directly costing you money or opportunities?

- Which health investments give you the highest energy ROI?

Wealth Habits Analysis

- Which wealth-generating activities add stress vs. reduce stress?

- Where does money stress damage your health?

---

2   For mechanical systems of habit-building, see James Clear's *Atomic Habits*. For energy management as performance optimization, see Jim Loehr's *The Power of Full Engagement*.

- Which wealth habits create more time and energy for health?
- How does financial stability improve your health decisions?

Integration Opportunities
- Where can you merge health and wealth activities?
- Which health practices would directly enhance your professional performance?
- What financial strategies could reduce health-harming stress?
- Where are you still treating health and wealth as competitors instead of complements?

Step 2: Compound Habit Identification

Identify Triple-Duty Habits (habits that serve multiple goals):
- Walking meetings → networking + exercise + creative thinking
- Meditation before calls → stress reduction + focus + decision quality
- Sunday meal prep → nutrition + time savings + reduced decision fatigue
- Morning routine → energy + productivity + stress management

Assessment Criteria
- Does this habit improve *both* health and wealth outcomes?
- Can it be sustained long-term without "perfect" conditions?
- Does it build positive momentum in multiple areas of life?
- What is the *minimum effective dose* for maximum benefit?

Step 3: Tracking Energy ROI

Define Your Own Metrics

Inputs (time/effort):
- Morning routine: ___ minutes
- Exercise: ___ minutes
- Meal prep: ___ minutes
- Other practices: ___ minutes

Outputs (performance impact):
- Focus quality: 1–10

- Daily energy levels: 1–10
- Stress resilience: 1–10
- Decision clarity: 1–10

Track for 30 Days:

- Which practices give the greatest energy return?
- Where do you hit diminishing returns?
- Which pairings work better than solo habits?
- How do health improvements directly affect work performance?

Step 4: Designing the Integration System

Build Your Health-Wealth Stack

Morning Integration:

- One habit to prime your body (e.g., movement, hydration)
- One habit to prime your mind (e.g., meditation, journaling)
- One habit that boosts both health and productivity

Workday Integration:

- Movement that fuels creativity (walking meetings, standing desk)
- Nutrition that stabilizes energy (strategic fasting, brain-focused foods)
- Stress management for decision-making (breathing, micro-meditations)

Recovery Integration:

- Evening routines that set up next-day performance
- Weekend activities that recharge for the work week
- Long-term compounding health practices (sleep, training, financial systems)

Measurement System

- Weekly: Energy assessment
- Monthly: Performance correlation analysis
- Quarterly: Optimize your system based on results

Your health-wealth stack isn't about "balance." It's about integration. Build one system that multiplies both, and you'll never have to trade one for the other again.

Wrapping It Up

You can't build a dream life on a broken foundation. Health is that foundation—the fuel that makes every other stack work. But health isn't separate from wealth creation. It's what makes wealth sustainable.

The richer your health, the richer your energy, decisions, relationships, and opportunities. The stronger your wealth systems, the more freedom and resources you have to reinvest in health. Stack them together, and you create compound returns that reinforce each other.

Start with habits that pull double duty. Choose routines that boost both energy and effectiveness. Build systems where self-care isn't a luxury—it's a force multiplier for the value you bring to others. That's how you create a life that grows stronger over time instead of burning out.

Now that we've locked in how to merge health and wealth into a single system, let's shift to a new challenge: preserving your skills so they don't atrophy, but instead become assets you can count on for life.

Further Reading

Cabo, Rafael de, and Mark P. Mattson. 2019. "Effects of Intermittent Fasting on Health, Aging, and Disease." *New England Journal of Medicine* 381 (26): 2541–51. https://doi.org/10.1056/nejmra1905136.

Jain, Manvi, and C. M. Markan. 2022. *Effect of Brief Meditation Intervention on Attention: An ERP Investigation*. arXiv. https://doi.org/10.48550/ARXIV.2209.12625.

Khodadad Kashi, Sholeh, Zahra Sadat Mirzazadeh, and Vahid Saatchian. 2022. "A Systematic Review and Meta-Analysis of Resistance Training on Quality of Life, Depression, Muscle Strength, and Functional Exercise Capacity in Older Adults Aged 60 Years or More." *Biological Research For Nursing* 25 (1): 88–106. https://doi.org/10.1177/10998004221120945.

Laukkanen, Jari A., Tanjaniina Laukkanen, and Setor K. Kunutsor. 2018. "Cardiovascular and Other Health Benefits of Sauna Bathing: A Review of the Evidence." *Mayo Clinic Proceedings* 93 (8): 1111–21. https://doi.org/10.1016/j.mayocp.2018.04.008.

Laukkanen, Tanjaniina, Hassan Khan, Francesco Zaccardi, and Jari A. Laukkanen. 2015. "Association Between Sauna Bathing and Fatal Cardiovascular and All-Cause Mortality Events." *JAMA Internal Medicine* 175 (4): 542. https://doi.org/10.1001/jamainternmed.2014.8187.

CHAPTER 18
THE SKILL PRESERVATION SYSTEM

What we learn to do, we learn by doing. Excellence, then, is not an act but a habit.

—Aristotle

Christopher had been crushing it as a software architect for three years—leading complex projects, mentoring junior developers, earning top performance reviews. On paper, everything was perfect. Yet something gnawed at him.

"I feel like I'm losing myself," he told his mentor Reese over coffee. "I haven't picked up my guitar in months. I used to be good—bands, original songs, even an album. Now I can barely remember basic chords."

Reese tilted her head. "Why does that bother you? You're thriving in your career."

"Because music was part of who I was. It gave me creativity, rhythm, and a sense of teamwork. Now I'm just…a code monkey. Honestly, my work feels more mechanical since I stopped feeding that creative side."

"So music skills actually helped your programming?"

Christopher paused. "Yeah. The best code has rhythm, flow, improvisation within limits. Back when I was playing, my architecture felt more elegant. I could *sense* when something was off, even before I could explain it."

Reese nodded. "Sounds like you don't need to choose between career and guitar. You need a skill preservation system. One that keeps old skills alive so they still fuel your work."

"But I barely have time for work as it is," Christopher protested.

"That's the wrong question. What if staying sharp on guitar *made you better* at work? What if 30 minutes of music gave you more insight than 30 minutes of extra coding?"

Skeptical but curious, Christopher agreed to Reese's challenge: pick one song he once loved, practice it 15 minutes every other day. Not to learn something new—just to keep the muscle memory alive.

That night, he pulled out his dusty acoustic guitar. Out of tune. Awkward in his hands. He chose *Blackbird* by The Beatles—a song that once flowed effortlessly, equal parts technical fingerpicking and melodic grace.

The first week was humbling. His fingers stumbled across changes that used to be second nature. Timing off. Flow gone. It was like trying to recall a language he used to speak fluently but hadn't practiced in years.

By week two, something clicked. The progressions started to flow. His fingers remembered their old pathways. But the real surprise came after practice: his afternoon coding sessions felt sharper, more creative. He saw patterns in software architecture he'd been missing.

Christopher didn't just get his music back—he got his edge back.

By week four, Christopher was hooked. Not on becoming a musician again, but on the way music practice was enhancing everything else. He experimented with timing, songs, and approaches. Sometimes he'd improvise chord progressions between meetings. Other times he'd tackle intricate fingerpicking while working through algorithmic problems.

The breakthrough came during a brutal project redesign. Christopher was stuck on how to organize a complex data flow system. That night, while grinding through a Bach piece, the answer hit. The way the musical phrases built on each other—repetition, variation, layered complexity—that was exactly how the system needed to be structured.

He spent the weekend reworking the architecture using principles of musical composition: themes, variations, callbacks, harmonic flow. On Monday, he unveiled it. The team was stunned at the elegance and clarity.

Three months later, Christopher reported back to Reese. "You were right. My guitar came back faster than I thought. But more importantly, my code improved. Keeping music alive improved the way I think everywhere else."

Reese smiled. "What shifted, specifically?"

"I started treating code like composition. My designs became more structured, more graceful. The team even said they were easier to follow. Turns out creativity isn't locked to one field—it transfers."

*
**

Just as Christopher learned, letting old skills die doesn't free up space—it weakens your edge. Many of the abilities you've sidelined as "irrelevant" could actually sharpen your performance today.

In this chapter, you'll learn how to preserve and cross-pollinate your skill stacks so they build on each other instead of competing.

The Drums That Saved My Business Thinking

You can spend years building a skill—then watch it waste away like an unused muscle.

It's not your imagination. It's called skill half-life. And if you're serious about stacking skills, you'd better learn how to beat it.

I learned this the hard way.

Drumming was my identity for more than twenty years. Rhythm wasn't just something I played—it was how I *thought*. I could read complex patterns at a glance, coordinate movements instinctively, and feel timing in my bones. It shaped how I saw everything from crowd dynamics to negotiations.

Then my life shifted. Trading education took off. Consulting clients multiplied. Boardrooms replaced drum kits.

At first, I didn't notice the decline. I was too busy stacking new skills, building new streams, expanding into new domains.

But then the decay showed up. My timing slipped on the few gigs I still played. Coordination wasn't automatic. Worse, my *business rhythm* dulled too. Reading crowds, sensing timing in deals, feeling the pulse of a room, all of it became mechanical.

That's when I realized: skills don't fade in isolation. They're connected. When one weakens, others suffer too.

Skills Fade Faster Than You Think

Skills are rocket fuel. They open doors, create leverage, shape your future.

But they all share one brutal flaw: if you don't use them, they decay. Have you ever tried to speak a language you haven't touched in years? Have you picked up an instrument you used to know, only to fumble later on? Have you opened a platform or software you used to dominate and felt like a beginner?

That's skill half-life. And the curve is cruel. Decay isn't slow or gentle—it's steep, fast, merciless. That's how the brain works. We forget what we do not practice.

The Two Strategies That Save You

If you want to stack skills *and* keep them, you have two options: Archive them and/or Integrate them.

Let's break it down.

Archiving: Safeguarding Your Assets

Archiving protects skills you don't use daily but may need to revive later. I learned this the hard way.

When my business was scaling fast, I wasn't creating new marketing systems every day. Some things were monthly, some seasonal, some only when we launched a new set for the band. At first, I left those systems up to memory. But I quickly realized that by hoping to remember them, I was leaving my valuable skills up to chance. It occurred to me: start documenting everything—spreadsheets, check-lists, workflows, CRM templates.

This went against my natural grain. I'm a creative and not a spreadsheet aficionado. I'm not naturally organized—far from it. But I'm too lazy to reinvent the wheel: archiving let my *future self* pick up where my past self left off.

Archiving meant:

- Creating cheat sheets for your future self
- Capturing steps, procedures, and reminders
- Making it easy to relaunch a skill with minimal ramp-up

Examples:

- Saved CRM workflows for lead generation and follow-up
- Step-by-step Google Drive files for event marketing
- Quick-start guides for old systems I might revive

I don't trust my memory. I built a reliable storage system for my knowledge.

Integration: Keep the Pot Simmering

Some skills are too valuable to let freeze. That's where integration comes in.

Integration means weaving skills into your life—even lightly—so they never go completely cold. It doesn't have to be daily. But it does have to be deliberate.

Examples:

- Play drums at home even if I'm not gigging every weekend
- Write landing page copy now and then, even off-cycle
- Rehearse presentations—even if I don't have a class that month

Small reps keep big skills alive. Think of it like keeping a pot on simmer instead of letting it go ice cold. When the time comes, you're ready.

What Happens When You Archive and Integrate

Master a skill, then safeguard it through archiving and integration, and you unlock:

- **Stress-free access:** Old skills return fast because you stored the blueprint
- **Adaptability:** You can jump into new roles, industries, or opportunities without starting from scratch
- **Compounding advantage:** You stack faster because you're not leaking hard-won proficiency

In a turbulent world, *skill agility is your insurance policy.*

Real Talk: If You Don't, You'll Pay the Price

I've seen it firsthand:

- Realtors who crushed it in the 2000s but can't run an Instagram ad today
- Musicians who took a break and lost their edge
- Entrepreneurs who outsourced sales until they forgot how to sell themselves

They didn't lose talent. They lost reps. And in a crisis—or a pivot—reps are what count.

The Skill Preservation Pyramid

Most people manage skills like hoarders—collecting random abilities, letting valuable ones decay, or obsessing over perfection in areas that don't move the needle.

I needed a system that would keep my stacks alive without burning me out or spreading me thin. That's why I built the Skill Preservation Pyramid—a three-tier strategy that organizes skills so you can protect past investments while still advancing.

Think of it as a strategic filing system for your abilities.

- **Level 1: Archive (The Safety Net)**
  A documented repository of every skill you've developed. Stored, mapped, and ready to reactivate when needed.

- **Level 2: Integration (The Essentials)**
  Light, consistent practice to keep your most transferable skills alive. Enough reps to prevent decay, without consuming your bandwidth.

- **Level 3: Growth (The Rocket Fuel)**
  Deep focus on 1–2 skills that directly advance your current mission. This is where intensity and mastery live.

The pyramid keeps your foundation of skills wide while sharpening your edge at the top.

When industries collapse, relationships shift, or health forces a pivot, your archived skills act as lifelines, your integrated essentials become bridges, and your growth skills provide rocket fuel for the next phase.

Your future self will thank you when the next crucible strikes. This is because you'll be stacked, stored, and ready to climb out.

Level 3
Prioritize Growth (Peak)
Focus intensive development on 1-2 skills that serve your current goals

Level 2
Integrate Essentials (Core)
Keep your most transferable skills warm with ongoing light practice

Level 1
Archive Everything (Foundation)
Document the skills you're not using actively but might need later

Level 1: Archive Everything

This is your **skill insurance policy.** You're not practicing these skills daily, but you're protecting your ability to revive them quickly.

What to archive:

- Step-by-step procedures for complex tasks

- Contact lists and network maps

- Templates and frameworks you've created

- Key learning resources and references

- Personal examples and case studies

How I archive:

- Electronic folders sorted by skill area (Marketing, Performance, Trading, etc.)

- Voice memos capturing the thought process on successful projects

- Screenshot portfolios of campaigns, presentations, or systems

- Relationship maps: who taught me what, and who I can re-engage with

- Simple checklists distilling complex processes into repeatable steps

Example: You've heard enough FlashPants stories to know this one—when we weren't touring during COVID, I kept detailed records of our booking process, venue contacts, pricing, and marketing templates. When the band came roaring back, I didn't have to start from scratch.

Level 2: Integrate Essentials

These are too valuable to let go cold. You keep them warm with light, regular practice.

What to integrate (Skills that cut across domains):

- Communication and presentation

- Pattern recognition and analytical thinking

- Creative problem-solving

- Relationship-building and networking

- Core technical skills in your profession

How I integrate them:

- Drumming: 20 minutes, twice weekly—songs I enjoy, not drills
- Writing: Daily journaling + occasional blogs, even when not working on a book
- Sales: Treating every client meeting as sales practice
- Teaching: Explaining concepts to team members, friends, or family
- Performance: Bringing stage presence into business presentations

Rule: Make it fun. If it feels like a chore, you won't sustain it.

Level 3: Prioritize Growth

This is where your concentrated development goes. Typically no more than 1–2 skills at a time.

Examples of my growth focus by season:

- *2018–2020:* Scaling entertainment + business systems
- *2020–2022:* Financial + trading education
- *2023–present:* Continued teaching + book writing + consulting + inventing + public speaking

How to pick growth priorities:

- What skills would 10x your current opportunities?
- Which align with your existing model?
- Which excite you enough to sustain deep practice?
- Which magnify the value of other skills you already have?

Keep in mind the 80/20 rule of skills: 80% of skill-building time goes to current priorities. 20% goes to archiving + integration.

How Skill Preservation Carries Over to Everything

Career Transitions

- Archived marketing knowledge = leverage when consulting
- Integrated communication = transferable to any new role
- Preserved networks = doors into multiple industries

Relationship Building

- Archive shared memories and milestones
- Integrate consistent check-ins with important people
- Prioritize deepening your top relationships

Financial Preparation

- Archive investment research + decision models
- Integrate routine practices for tracking + review
- Prioritize learning strategies that fit current goals

The Skill Preservation Pyramid keeps your foundation wide, your essentials sharp, and your growth targeted. That's how you avoid atrophy and build agility for whatever comes next.

The Integration Multiplier Effect

Here's what most people miss: when you carry old skills into new contexts, you don't just *preserve* them—you multiply them.

My intersections:

- **Drumming + Business:** Rhythm and timing sharpen my ability to read room energy in meetings and know when to push or pull back in negotiations.

- **Performance + Teaching:** Stage presence and crowd-reading translate directly into classroom management and student engagement.

- **Sales + Consulting:** FlashPants booking and YPAR Firm client development taught me how to surface needs and articulate value in high-ticket consulting.

- **Systems Thinking + Health:** The same process optimization I used in business helps me build sustainable health routines and habits.

The magic is always at the **intersections.** Preserved skills cross-pollinate and create new capabilities you could never reach by specializing in one domain alone.

Why Most People Fail at Skill Preservation

- **They treat it like homework, not investment.**
  Skill upkeep is like gardening—small, regular care—not cramming for a test.

- **They try to maintain everything equally.**
  Impossible. You can't give the same energy to every skill. The pyramid solves this by assigning levels.

- **They fail to link old skills to new goals.**
  If you can't see the connection, you'll drop it. Look harder for how an old skill feeds your current direction.

- **They confuse activity with practice.**
  Reading about guitar isn't playing guitar. Thinking about networking isn't actually connecting. Real reps are the only reps that count.

Chapter 18 Activity: Your Skill Preservation System

Time to build your personal system for keeping skills alive while still stacking new ones. Follow this four-step analysis: audit your current skills, design your pyramid, set your integration plan, and build your skill library.

Step 1: Skill Decay Audit

Skills at Risk

- What abilities have you used regularly in the past but rarely use now?

- Which skills you worked hard to acquire are starting to rust?

- Where do you see performance drop compared to your peak?

- What might you need again but aren't practicing today?

Impact Evaluation

- Which fading skills could limit future opportunities?

- Where could skill loss be quietly hurting current performance?

- What skills do people still associate with you that you're not maintaining?

- Which decaying skills could amplify your current focus if revived?

Step 2: Pyramid Design

Archive (Base Layer)

List 5–8 skills to record and store:

- Skills not used daily but worth saving

- Complex procedures you'll forget if not captured

- Domain knowledge and key networks

- Frameworks, systems, or processes you've built

Integration (Core Layer)

Select 3–4 skills for light, regular practice:

- Transferable across multiple domains

- Energizing and easy to maintain

- Complementary to your current priorities

- High utility for low time investment

Growth (Peak Layer)

Choose 1–2 skills for deep focus:

- Which would 10x your opportunities?

- Which align with your business model or mission?

- Which excite you enough to sustain practice?

- Which make other skills more valuable?

Step 3: Integration Strategy

Weekly Integration Plan

For each core skill, define:

- *Minimum effective dose:* What's the smallest practice that keeps it alive?

- *Natural contexts:* Where can you practice while doing other things?

- *Enjoyment factor:* How do you keep it fun, not a chore?

- *Transfer opportunities:* Where can this skill improve existing projects?

Example Schedule

- **Monday:** 20 minutes drumming along to music I enjoy

- **Wednesday:** Voice memo reflection (writing practice) during commute

- **Friday:** A natural networking chat, seamlessly woven into the normal flow of business, while sitting at the bar of my favorite fine dining spot. It's stacking fun, enjoying great food in amazing venues while building connections. A true win-win-win.

- **Weekend:** Creative problem-solving session on a personal project

Step 4: Create Your Skill Library

Digital Organization

- Folders by skill area
- Cheat sheets for detailed processes
- Contact lists + relationship maps
- Templates, frameworks, and references

Retrieval System

- Searchable naming conventions
- Regular review (quarterly or bi-annual)
- Quick-start guides for a fast refresh
- Progress tracking for integrated skills

Maintenance Rhythm

- **Weekly:** Practice integrated skills
- **Monthly:** Review and update priorities
- **Quarterly:** Archive new skills + evaluate decay risks
- **Annually:** Full pyramid reset and reconfiguration

Do this once, and you'll never watch hard-earned skills slip away again. Archive what you don't use, integrate what matters, and grow what matters most. That's how you keep your edge for life.

Wrapping It Up

You don't build the future by abandoning the past. You build it by preserving what matters while focusing on what's next.

The Skill Preservation System doesn't make you a jack-of-all-trades. It makes you a strategic generalist, someone who keeps access to a wide range of abilities while sharpening concentrated expertise.

- **Archived skills** become paths you keep open
- **Integrated skills** become advantages
- **Priority skills** become superpowers

Most people treat skill development like a straight line: add something new, drop something old. Real stackers build like pyramid builders. They keep a broad base while pushing higher at the top. The goal isn't to be excellent at everything—it's to stay *dangerous* in many domains and *dominant* in a few.

Start simple. Pick one skill you've been letting atrophy. Archive it properly or integrate it lightly. Then build from there.

Because the future doesn't belong to the person who *used to have it*. It belongs to the one who still does.

Now that we've locked in how to maintain your skill stacks, it's time to explore the other side of mastery: knowing when to say *no* so you can protect the power to say *yes* to what matters most.

THE POWER OF NO (AND LETTING THE RIGHT YES FIND YOU)

The difference between successful people and very successful people is that very successful people say no to almost everything.

—Warren Buffett

Owen had been the "yes guy" for three straight years. *Yes* to every client project—even the ones that paid peanuts. *Yes* to every networking event—even when he was exhausted. *Yes* to every favor from friends who treated his time like it was free.

"I don't get why I'm so burned out," he told his coach Blake over coffee. "I'm working 70 hours a week, my schedule's slammed, but my bank account isn't moving. I feel like I'm running in circles."

Blake leaned back. "Walk me through your week."

"Monday I've got three client calls, then that startup networking thing downtown. Tuesday I've got a nonprofit board meeting I can't miss, plus two client projects. Wednesday—"

"Hold up," Blake said. "What did you say *no* to this week?"

Owen froze. "Nothing, I guess. People depend on me."

"Do they?" he asked. "Or are you just afraid to disappoint anyone?"

The question hit like a punch to the gut. Owen couldn't remember the last time he'd said *no* to anything.

Blake slid his notebook across the table. "Here's your assignment. For one week, say *no* to one thing every day. Doesn't matter what: a meeting, a social invite, a favor. Just practice the word."

"But what if I miss something important?"

"Owen, you're already missing something important: the chance to do *great* work because you're too scattered. Every yes to something mediocre is a *no* to something extraordinary."

Day one, a prospective client asked for a rush job at half Owen's normal rate. Old Owen would've jumped. New Owen said: "That deadline won't work for me, but I can deliver excellent work in two weeks at my regular rate."

The client said yes.

By week three, Owen had turned down six low-fit projects, declined three dead-end networking meetings, and quit a volunteer committee that drained his energy.

The result? His existing clients got better work. His energy returned. And his revenues jumped 30%.

"The strange thing," he told Blake a month later, "is that people respect me more now. When you're selective, your yes actually means something. I'm not the desperate guy anymore—I'm the one who only takes on projects I can crush."

*
**

As Owen discovered, strategic *noes* create space for strategic *yeses*. If you're saying yes to everything and wondering why nothing adds up, this chapter will show you how *no* becomes your sharpest tool for focus, for respect, and for the success you actually want.

The Yes Trap I Fell Into

I was the king of *yes* in my early years.

- *Yes* to gigs we undercharged for.
- *Yes* to clients who drained my energy.
- *Yes* to relationships that didn't serve me.
- *Yes* to tasks I didn't want—just to feel needed.

Here's what I learned the hard way: every *yes* is also a *no*.

A *no* to your energy. A *no* to your goals. A *no* to your future.

Saying *no* isn't rejection; it's a filter, a skill that compounds. And once you learn it, everything changes.

Why No Is Really a Success Skill

Most people avoid *no* because they're afraid. Afraid to disappoint. Afraid to miss out. Afraid to burn a bridge. But *no* is one of the most strategic moves you can make. When you say *no* to the wrong thing, you clear the runway for the right one. It's not just about boundaries. It's about precision.

Saying *no* taught me that it is truly a skill. You develop your ability to focus when you regularly reject distractions. You earn respect from those around you who recognize that you value both your time and theirs. You save countless hours that would have gone to needless busywork, meaningless events, or downright unwise commitments. And finally, saying *no* paradoxically frees you to say *yes* to the real opportunities that will shape your future in a positive way.

The No That Changed Everything

At one point I was teaching part-time, still running the band, stretched thin. Then I was invited to take on another side project.

Old me would've jumped. More money, nice people, new project. But I paused. I asked myself: *Does this serve where I'm going, or does it pull me off track?*

That single *no* freed up the bandwidth I needed to prep for, and crush, my audition to become a full-time financial educator. That yes reshaped my entire career. And it only came because I was willing to say *no* first.

The Compound Effect of Strategic Noes

Every time you say *no* to something that doesn't fit, you create space. And that space always fills—with something better.

- I said *no* to a draining band schedule… and yes to a speaking career.
- I said *no* to toxic people… and yes to healthier partnerships.
- I said *no* to poor-fit clients… and yes to higher-paying, easier ones.

Each *no* stacked on the last—until it built a life that finally made sense.

How to Say No Without Burning Bridges

Define Your Yes First

If you don't know what you *do* want, you'll keep saying yes to everything else. Ask yourself: What am I building? What truly matters right now?

Keep It Simple

You don't owe anyone a 20-minute explanation. Short, direct phrases are enough:

- "Thanks for considering me, but I'll have to decline."
- "That's not a fit for me right now."
- "I'm not available, but thanks for asking."

Provide an Alternative Where Possible

A *no* paired with a helpful redirect still adds value:

- "I'm not able to, but I know someone who'd be perfect."
- "I'm out on this one, but keep me posted if something like X comes up again."

Practice Small Noes

Your *no* muscles grow with reps, so start small:

- Decline a meeting that doesn't need you.
- Skip a dinner you're not into.
- Reclaim your time, step by step.

Scan for a handy guide on ways to say *no* without burning bridges:

How No Skills Apply to Everything

Business Development

How they transfer:

- *no* to clients who don't value your expertise means yes to high-end pricing
- *no* to scope creep means *yes* to profitable projects
- *no* to random networking means *yes* to strategic relationship building

Examples:

- A consultant who stops taking rush jobs at discount rates suddenly attracts clients who plan ahead and pay full price.
- A freelancer who declines projects outside her niche becomes the go-to expert in her field.

Health and Fitness

How they transfer:

- *no* to junk food = yes to stable energy
- *no* to skipping workouts = yes to long-term strength
- *no* to all-or-nothing thinking = yes to sustainable habits

Examples:

- Saying *no* to late-night snacking opens the door for more sleep and better mornings
- Avoiding drinking-based social events creates space for activities that actually energize you. (If you do attend an event with alcohol present, a club soda with lime should get you through the event relatively unscathed)

Relationships

How they transfer:

- *no* to drama and energy vampires = yes to meaningful connection
- *no* to people-pleasing = yes to authenticity
- *no* to relationships based on what you do = yes to ones based on who you are

Examples:

- Setting boundaries with family members who constantly stir drama protects your energy for healthy relationship.

- Declining requests from people who only reach out when they need something frees you for true friendships

Reinvention Skill Highlight: Strategic Filtering

Why *no* matters: it shifts life design from collecting experiences to curating them.

Here's how to stack it:

1. **Audit Your Current *Yeses*:** List every commitment. Ask: *Would I sign up for this again today?*

2. **Practice Micro-*noes*:** Start with small declines—one meeting, one invitation, one favor

3. **Create Decision Criteria:** Define 3–5 conditions that must be true before you say yes to new opportunities

4. **Monitor the Results:** Track what actually happens when you say *no*. *Spoiler*: the feared fallout usually doesn't happen

5. **Celebrate the Space:** Notice what opens up when you're not overcommitted. That space is where your best work lives

Chapter 19 Activity: Your Strategic No Practice

Time to start building your *no* muscle on purpose.

Step 1: Current Yes Audit

List every commitment you're carrying right now:

- Work projects and responsibilities

- Social commitments and recurring meetings

- Personal habits and routines

- Relationship obligations

For each, ask:

- Does this give me energy or drain me?

- Is it moving me toward my main goals?
- Would I commit to this again if asked today?

Step 2: Design Your *No* Scripts

Craft 3–5 clear, courteous ways to decline:

- **Work:** "I'm not accepting any more projects this quarter."
- **Social:** "Thanks for the invite, but I'm not available."
- **Routine favors:** "That's not something I can take on right now."
- **Alternative:** "I can't do X, but [person/resource] might be a fit."

Write them down. Practice until they roll off your tongue.

Step 3: Define Your *Yes* Criteria

Set 3–5 rules that something must meet before you agree:

- Aligns with my top 3 priorities
- Energizes me instead of draining me
- I can do it well without sacrificing existing commitments
- It builds toward my long-term vision
- The person/opportunity has earned access to my time

If it doesn't meet these criteria, it's a *no*. Simple.

Step 4: The Weekly *No* Challenge

This week, say *no* three times:

1. Decline one small request that isn't aligned with your priorities.
2. Turn down one social invite that feels like obligation, not joy.
3. Refuse or delegate one work task that doesn't need your hands on it.

Then track: How did you feel? What did you do with the reclaimed time and energy?

Wrapping It Up

You don't have to say yes to everything. In fact, you shouldn't. Say yes to everything, and you dilute your energy, your time, your attention. What *no* actually does is make you intentional.

So the next time something comes along and you feel that pull in your gut: the quiet signal that says *this isn't it*, trust it. Say *no* and create space for the bigger yes that's still on its way.

Your future self will thank you for protecting the sanctuary where your most important work gets done.

CHAPTER 20
MANIFESTATION WITHOUT THE HYPE

What you think you create. What you feel you attract.
And what you imagine you become.

—*The Buddha*

Before we dive in, let me clear something up. People describe this principle in different ways. Some call it God's design; some call it the subconscious mind; others call it universal law. I'm not here to argue labels. What matters is that the mechanism works the same no matter what worldview you bring to the table: what you accept inwardly is what gets expressed outwardly.

This principle isn't new. It's been taught for centuries in different forms—through Scripture, through philosophy, and through modern psychology. The wording changes, but the essence is always the same: *the inner world shapes the outer world.*

Naomi thought she was manifesting. Vision boards covered her walls. Affirmations filled her mirror. Every morning she visualized her dream life—financial freedom, the perfect relationship, the thriving business.

But nothing happened.

"I don't get it," she told her therapist, Dr. Valecourt. "I think positive. I visualize. I practice gratitude. But my life looks the same."

Valecourt leaned in. "When you visualize, what do you feel?"

"Incredible. I get so pumped. Sometimes I spend an hour daydreaming about how amazing it's going to be."

"And then?"

"Then I go to my boring job. It's like a crash—back to reality."

Valecourt nodded. "That's the problem. Excitement keeps it in the future. You don't need a high—you need to assume it. If you felt it as real now, your inner mind would have no choice but to express it."

So Naomi shifted. Instead of hyping herself about her "future business," she assumed its present reality. She imagined the simple, ordinary details—logging into her bank account, answering customer emails, even sighing through tax season. She carried the *feeling of already being the woman who owned a thriving business.*

Three months later, she launched her first product. Six months later, she cleared her first five-figure month.

And it didn't feel like magic. It felt natural. Obvious. Inevitable.

*
**

The Manifestation Mistake Most People Make

Let's get one thing straight: most manifestation advice is empty calories.

- "Think good thoughts and the universe will provide!"
- "Just believe harder and it will happen!"
- "Make a vision board and watch your dreams appear!"

Nonsense. But beneath the fluff lies a law that is unbreakable: whatever you impress upon the inner mind in feeling, it must express.

Call it the subconscious. Call it the way God wired us. Call it universal law. The label doesn't matter. The principle does: your life isn't shaped by wishful thinking—it's shaped by what you *feel as true right now.*

How This Book Became Real

Before I wrote a single word, this book already existed.

Not as a dream of bestseller lists. Not as a fantasy of TV interviews or keynotes.

I simply assumed it. I imagined it sitting on my nightstand—pages bent from use, a tea ring on the cover, as ordinary as brushing my teeth. That quiet assumption was enough. My inner world accepted it as fact. From there, the writing unfolded naturally.

Not thrilling. Not suspenseful. Just inevitable.

Why Excitement Blocks the Process

Excitement keeps desire at arm's length.

- If the state feels thrilling, giddy, and "someday," your mind treats it as fantasy.
- If the state feels natural, routine, and assumed, your mind treats it as fact.

The inner self does not argue, reason, or question. It simply expresses what is impressed upon it. And the only language it understands is feeling.

You don't manifest what excites you. You manifest what you accept as already true.

Scripture echoes the same idea: "Faith is the substance of things hoped for, the evidence of things not seen" (Hebrews 11:1). Whether you take that as divine truth or practical psychology, the meaning is the same—what you accept inwardly becomes your outer reality.

The Three Principles That Actually Work

This approach to manifestation can be condensed into three working principles:

Principle 1: Assume the End, Not the Process

Don't obsess over how it will happen. The "how" belongs to forces beyond your conscious control.

- Wrong: "I can't wait until I finally hit six figures—it'll be amazing!"
- Right: "I feel the calm certainty of already being a six-figure earner."

Practice: Construct a short, ordinary scene that implies the wish is fulfilled—a bank statement, a conversation, a detail of daily life. Then step into the *feeling of that scene being real right now.*

Principle 2: Use Sleep and Prayer as Gateways

Your last waking mood is the seed that drops into the subconscious. Don't fall asleep rehearsing frustration or lack.

Before bed, replay your chosen scene. Feel its reality until it carries you into sleep. This is the most powerful time to impress the subconscious.

Prayer works the same way. Not begging, not wishing, but assuming: "Thank you—it is done." Jesus said it plainly: "Therefore I tell you, whatever you ask for in prayer, believe that you have received it, and it will be yours" (Mark 11:24). Beyond Scripture, psychology tells us something identical: your mind accepts what you feel as real.

Principle 3: Live in the Spirit of the State

Every state of being has a mood. Wealth feels different than struggle. Love feels different than loneliness.

The task is to live in the spirit of your desired state—not sometimes, not only in meditation, but through the day. When doubt or old identity creeps up, redirect: *"No—that's not who I am anymore. This is who I am now."*

The subconscious always expresses the dominant feeling. Make the desired state your dominant mood, and life must rearrange to match it.

How Manifestation Transfers to Everything

This isn't limited to "big life goals." The same law of assumption applies in every domain: business, health, skill-building, even daily habits.

Business Development

How it transfers:

- Construct a simple scene: a client shaking your hand, or a payment notification.
- Enter the feeling: calm certainty that your work is valued and well-compensated.
- Each night before sleep, replay that scene until it feels natural.
- By day, carry yourself in the spirit of someone who already operates a successful business.

Example:
A consultant no longer imagines "someday working with great clients." Instead, she falls asleep each night feeling the satisfaction of having just signed one. Within months, ideal clients flow to her naturally.

Health and Fitness

How it transfers:

- Construct the scene: lacing your shoes for a workout, hearing your doctor say, "You're in excellent health."

- Feel the relief and satisfaction of already being healthy.

- Sow this feeling nightly. Prayer during the day is simple gratitude: "Thank you, this is who I am now."

- Live in the spirit of vitality—your actions will flow from that state without strain.

Example:
Instead of fantasizing about a dramatic transformation, one man assumed that he was fit now. Each night, he replayed the mental scene of himself jogging lightly and feeling strong. Soon his choices—meals, workouts, lifestyle—aligned naturally, without friction.

Skill Development

How it transfers:

- Construct the scene: solving a coding problem, finishing a song, or having a fluent conversation.

- Enter the feeling of competence—not hype, but ordinary ability.

- Fall asleep with that assumption, letting the subconscious rehearse it overnight.

- Carry the mood of "I am skilled" during the day, and your practice takes on the quality of mastery.

Example:
A beginner programmer stopped dreaming about being a tech genius and instead envisioned himself already solving problems with code. Night after night, he rehearsed this end. Within months, his skills accelerated beyond what grinding alone had produced.

Chapter 20 Activity: The Assumption Practice

Now it's your turn. Don't just read—practice.

Step 1: Construct Your End Scene

Pick one goal. Imagine a **short, ordinary scene** that would only be true if your desire were already fulfilled.

Step 2: Enter the Feeling of Fulfillment

Replay the scene slowly. Don't just see it—**feel it.** Relief, calm, gratitude.

Step 3: Nightly Rehearsal

Before bed, replay your scene and let it carry you into sleep. The subconscious accepts what you feel in that state.

Step 4: Prayer of Assumption

During the day, use prayer—not begging, but assumption: *"Thank you—it is already so."*

Step 5: Spirit Check Throughout the Day

Ask: *"What mood am I carrying right now?"* Redirect back to the state of fulfillment until it becomes second nature. Scan the code for an extensive guide on manifestation techniques:

Wrapping It Up

This isn't about forcing results. It's about impressing the subconscious with assumption until the outer world mirrors it.

- **Construct the end scene.**
- **Feel it fulfilled.**
- **Sow at night.**
- **Pray as if it's done.**
- **Carry the spirit daily.**

Do this, and manifestation doesn't feel like a miracle. It feels ordinary. Natural. Inevitable.

Whether you see it as faith in God's promises, or simply the mechanics of your inner mind, the law is the same: your outer world is nothing more than your inner assumptions pushed out.

CHAPTER 21
THE MASTER STACK

The whole is greater than the sum of its parts.

—Aristotle

Tabitha had spent two years collecting certificates. Sales training. Leadership seminars. Public speaking classes. Networking conferences. Productivity systems.

Her résumé was stacked. Her LinkedIn looked bulletproof. On paper, she was impressive.

But something was off.

"I have all these pieces," she told her coach, Peter, "but they don't add up. I'm good at sales, but my leadership feels stiff. I can speak on stage, but my networking comes off as forced. I've got systems for everything, but nothing flows."

Peter nodded. "That's because you've been collecting skills, not stacking them."

"What's the difference?"

"A collection is just parts sitting side by side. A stack is when those parts connect and multiply each other. Your sales ability should make your leadership more persuasive. Your speaking skills should make your networking magnetic. Your systems thinking should make everything else smoother."

Tabitha frowned. "So how do I make them work together?"

Peter smiled. "It's like cooking. You can have the best ingredients in the world, but if you don't combine them, all you have is raw stuff. Integration is where the magic happens."

He slid a notebook across the table. "Pick your top three strengths. Then find one project that forces you to use all three. Not separately, but together."

Tabitha thought for a moment. "I could lead a team project: sell the vision to stakeholders, present results to the public, and build systems to manage workflow."

"Perfect. Stop thinking: *now I'm selling, now I'm leading, now I'm organizing.* Instead, approach it as *I'm solving this challenge with all of me.* Let your skills talk to each other."

Tabitha tested it. She used sales to understand what clients needed, leadership to guide her team toward solutions, systems thinking to create repeatable processes, and clear speaking skills to present the results effectively.

The project crushed expectations. But more than that, Tabitha finally felt aligned. She wasn't a résumé of random skills. She was an integrated professional with her own style.

"The breakthrough," she told Peter, "wasn't adding new skills. It was learning to use the ones I already had, together."

*
**

Like Tabitha, you might already have more skills than you realize. The missing piece isn't acquisition. It's integration. This chapter will show you how to create your own Master Stack: the system where everything you've learned combines into something uniquely powerful, distinctly yours.

The Integration Moment

After fifteen years of building skills in drumming, sales, systems, healing arts, entertainment, education, and entrepreneurship, I hit a wall.

Not because I lacked talent. Rather, I had it scattered across interests and domains.

I was strong at individual things but weak at weaving them together. A chef with a world-class pantry, but always serving one-ingredient dishes.

The epiphany came during a brutal consulting assignment. The client needed someone who could:

- Analyze a broken lead-generation system (systems thinking)
- Design creative solutions (problem-solving + creativity)
- Present findings to skeptical executives (performance + teaching)
- Win over resistant team members (sales + leadership)
- Build sustainable processes (systems design)

At first, I treated these as separate tasks. Then it hit me: they weren't separate at all. They were facets of the same solution. My skills weren't competing for airtime; they were designed to work in harmony.

That's when it clicked: a master stack isn't about collecting more skills. It's about getting the ones you already have to function as a single, integrated system—where the whole is exponentially more than the sum of its parts.

The Five Levels of Skill Integration

After years of trial, failure, and iteration, I've recognized five stages of development. Most people never move beyond Level Three. The master stack lives at Levels Four and Five.

Level 1: Skill Acquisition

Learning individual skills in isolation.

- *Example:* Taking a sales course, studying presentation skills, learning leadership theory.

This is where most people start—and quit. They collect skills like trophies without ever combining them.

Level 2: Skill Application

Using skills effectively in their intended contexts.

- *Example:* Being good at sales on sales calls, effective at presenting during a meeting, showing leadership in a team huddle.

This is competence—you can "do the job," but you still treat each skill as a separate tool.

Level 3: Skill Transfer

Applying skills across domains.

- *Example:* Using sales skills in job interviews, presentation skills in relationships, leadership skills in parenting.

This is where stacking begins. You see how tools overlap, not just how they work in silos.

Level 4: Skill Synthesis

Combining multiple skills simultaneously for compound effects.

- *Example:* Delivering a presentation that informs, persuades, entertains, builds trust, and resolves objections—all at once.

This is where exponential results start, where people become notable for their skillsets and talents.

Level 5: Skill Mastery

Your skills dissolve into a natural, unique approach.

- *Example:* Your problem-solving style is yours alone—not because you force a technique, but because your integrated stack produces an outcome nobody else can replicate.

This is mastery. You're no longer "using" skills. You've *become* them.

My Master Stack: The Integration Story

Here's how my skills fused over time into something bigger than the sum of their parts:

Early Integration: Real Estate + Entertainment + Business (2005-2017)

My skillset originally included drumming and plate slinging at Islands. But over time, I developed other skills as part of my stack, like sales, marketing, negotiation, and rudimentary business management. This combination became gasoline on the fire once we launched Flashpants. We weren't just musicians looking for a gig—we became entertainers who could scale. Revenue went from $0 to 200+ shows per year across multiple states and casts.

Advanced Integration: Teaching + Sales + Performance (2020–2022)

- **Education skills** (breaking down complexity)
- **Sales skills** (reading needs, creating urgency)
- **Performance skills** (commanding attention, managing energy) = **Financial education success**

I wasn't just teaching or selling; I was solving problems and driving results. That's how I shifted from band leader to business owner to educator. And my ability to understand what triggers a student's *aha* moment is what propelled me from teaching small classrooms to filling ever-larger ones.

Master Integration: All Skills Working Together (2023–Present)

At the highest level, our skills combine in interesting and powerful ways, if we know how to spot and use them. In my life:

Trading education continues as a core skill. I still teach intensive courses where performing keeps students engaged, where my entertainment background helps me spot what works and what doesn't, and where my time as a healer helps me meet learners where they are at. These skills in isolation—which is where most people leave theirs—aren't unique or especially in-demand. Together, these skills form a tapestry unique to me.

My consulting work draws from that same pool of experience and skills: my marketing, problem-solving, teaching, sales, performance, leadership, and relationship-building experience is precisely what clients pay for.

The writing of this book taps into the deepest reaches of my teaching, entertainment, storytelling, systems thinking, and personal development lessons—often hard won. But writing also has the unique quality of clarifying your beliefs, letting you condense many ideas into just the best ones. Many good writers have plenty of talent with putting pen to paper, but lack the experience and follow-through to actually publish a book. In the end, writing was not very different from knocking on thousands of doors: a little every day led to enormous results.

Public Speaking is an extension and expression of all these skills. My experiences do not sit behind glass. Instead, I share them regularly with students across the U.S. But I could not be an effective speaker if I did not have an intimate understanding of energy reading, crowd management, entertainment, business, and a memory of what it is like to be a total beginner.

Every facet of my life now pulls from the *whole stack* of skills that I've cultivated. Nothing is siloed; nothing is wasted. Surprisingly, the skills that I thought were useless or non-transferrable have been some of my strongest "secret weapons" when entering a new field.

That is the power of a Master Stack.

The Four Principles of Master Stack Creation

Principle 1: Identify Your Intersection Points

Find the overlap where your skills naturally work together.

- Don't ask, "How do I use my selling skills now?"
- Do ask, "What problem could be solved with *my entire skill stack*?"

My example: The intersection of entertainment, education, and business systems created opportunities pure educators, pure entertainers, or pure consultants couldn't reach.

Principle 2: Design Integrated Experiences

Stop doing one thing at a time. Build experiences that achieve multiple outcomes simultaneously.

Example: Teaching trading doesn't just educate. It builds relationships, demonstrates expertise, generates income, and creates content for later use.

Principle 3: Allow Skills to Inform One Another

Let your skills cross-pollinate. Each one should make the others stronger.

In my life:

- Performance skills make my teaching more engaging.
- Teaching skills make my business pitches more educational.
- Systems thinking makes my creative work scalable.

Principle 4: Develop Your Signature Approach

The endgame is a style no one else can copy—because no one else has your exact stack.

My example: Entertainment-based business education with systematic implementation. That signature approach didn't come from chasing trends. It came from my stack colliding into something only I could deliver.

How Master Stacks Transfer to Everything

Business Development

Stop saying, "I have to network" or "I have to sell." Start asking, "How can I add value with my entire stack?"

Examples:

- A graphic designer who merges design expertise + psychology background + business savvy → becomes a brand strategist creating visual identities that drive real outcomes.

- A former teacher who merges teaching expertise + tech skills + business knowledge → builds online courses that actually change behavior.

Career Development

Forget the conventional ladder. Build a role that only your stack can fill.

Examples:

- A project manager who combines organization + emotional intelligence + creative problem-solving → reinvents as a culture consultant repairing broken teams with better systems.

- An engineer who fuses technical skills + communication + business strategy → evolves into a "technical translator" who helps companies implement complex solutions.

Personal Relationships

Don't compartmentalize yourself. Bring your full stack into every interaction.

Examples:

- Teaching skills to help your partner understand your perspective, leadership to guide family decisions, creativity to resolve conflicts.

- Work problem-solving applied to personal issues, while relationship-building skills strengthen your professional network.

The Master Stack Evaluation Framework

Integration Audit

- What are your top five developed skills?
- Where do they naturally want to cooperate?
- What problems could only your unique combination solve?
- How could these strengths teach and strengthen each other?

Opportunity Identification

- What problems can *you* solve that others can't because of your stack?
- What unique value emerges when your competencies combine?
- Where are the market gaps tailor-made for your strengths?

Experience Design

- How can you structure opportunities to use multiple skills at once?
- What activities let you practice integration in real time?
- How can you design your work so that skills cross-pollinate instead of silo?

Signature Development

- What do you call it when your abilities operate together?
- How does your integrated approach differ from traditional approaches?
- What do people instantly recognize as *your* signature style of problem-solving?

Reinvention Skill Feature: Strategic Integration

The master stack is the ultimate reinvention skill. It transforms you from "skilled" into uniquely capable.

Here's how to stack this meta-skill:

- **Skill Inventory:** Map all your abilities—even the ones you take for granted
- **Integration Exercises:** Practice intentionally combining multiple skills in one setting

- **Opportunity Design:** Seek or create projects that demand your unique mix

- **Approach Development:** Observe how your skills collaborate and reinforce each other

- **Signature Evolution:** Continuously refine your holistic style based on outcomes and feedback

Chapter 21 Activity: Build Your Master Stack

Time to put everything you've learned together and design your own integrated system.

Step 1: Master Skill Inventory

Catalog your full stack across every area of life.

Professional Skills

- Technical capabilities you've developed through work

- Industry knowledge and experience

- Business and organizational abilities

Life Skills

- Communication and relationship skills

- Creative and artistic skills

- Physical and health-related skills

Learning Skills

- Analytical and problem-solving skills

- Teaching and mentoring abilities

- Skills for learning and adaptation

Hidden Skills

- Things you're good at but don't label as "skills"

- Abilities people often ask for your help with

- Natural strengths you take for granted

Step 2: Integration Mapping

Spot where your skills want to cooperate.

Skill Clusters

- Which skills already show up together in your work or life?
- What pairings could amplify each other if combined?
- Where do you see untapped synergies?

Unique Intersections

- What unusual combinations do you have that most people don't?
- What value could only your stack create?
- What problems can *you* solve because of your unique blend?

Step 3: Integration Experiment Design

Create practice opportunities to work your stack as a system.

Current Projects

- How could you reframe existing work to pull in more of your stack?
- What would change if you attacked challenges with *all* your skills at once?

New Experiments

- What project could you design that forces you to use 3+ skills simultaneously?
- Where could you generate new value using your unique mix?
- What opportunity would let you combine capabilities you've never tested together?

Step 4: Signature Approach Development

Define the method that emerges when your skills collaborate.

Approach Identification

- When you use your stack, what process naturally emerges?
- How does it differ from traditional approaches?
- What do others instantly recognize as "your way" of solving problems?

Value Proposition

- What outcomes can you deliver through integration that you couldn't with single skills?

- What unique results only happen when *all* your capabilities come together?

- How would you explain your holistic approach so others see its power?

Wrapping It Up

The master stack isn't about stockpiling skills. It's about weaving your skills together so tightly that you create capabilities nobody else can replicate.

When doing the work makes you a better teacher… When building simple routines helps you come up with better ideas… When knowing how to work with people improves the quality of what you build…

That's when you stop being "a person with skills" and become *uniquely capable.*

This is the ultimate reinvention—not just learning new things, but fusing everything you've learned into a style that's distinctly yours.

Start with what you already have. Find where your skills naturally want to collaborate. Create opportunities to practice integration. Pay attention to what emerges.

The master stack isn't a finish line. It evolves as you grow, learn, and find new intersections.

Your competitive edge isn't the list of skills you've acquired. It's the way you integrate them. That integration is your signature. That's the contribution no one else can copy.

That's your master stack.

CHAPTER 22
STOP IN-ORDER-TO-ING YOUR LIFE

How we spend our days is, of course, how we spend our lives.
—Annie Dillard

Jacob had been grinding for three years straight. Sixteen-hour days spent building his marketing company. No vacations. No hobbies. Barely any sleep. His apartment looked like a college dorm—takeout boxes, unmade bed, clothes strewn across the floor.

"I'll clean up when business slows down," he told his girlfriend, Rachel. "I'll take a vacation once I'm making six figures. I'll get in shape when things cal down. I'll call my parents when I have more time."

Rachel finally snapped. "Jacob, you're living like a monk who hates his monastery. When do you think *someday* is going to show up?"

"When I'm successful. When I've made it. When I don't have to worry about money anymore."

"And what's the magic number that will make you finally live?"

Jacob hesitated. He knew he'd been moving the goalposts for years. First $50K in revenue. Then $100K. Then $200K. Every milestone just opened up another one.

"You're in-order-to-ing your life away," Rachel said. "You're living in order to succeed, in order to relax, in order to enjoy yourself. But what if you never arrive? What if you spend your entire life *getting ready to live* instead of actually living?"

The words rattled him. That weekend, instead of working, Jacob cleaned his apartment—really cleaned it. He bought fresh flowers. Cooked dinner instead of ordering takeout. Called his parents—something he'd put off for longer than he liked to admit—and talked for two hours.

Monday morning, something surprising happened. His work was sharper. Client calls were more efficient. He felt more creative in his side business.

"It's crazy," he admitted to Rachel. "I thought taking time to live would hurt my business. But I'm performing better."

Six months later, Jacob didn't just hit his revenue targets—he blew past them. His secret wasn't more hours. It was working from fullness, not emptiness.

"The breakthrough," he told Rachel, "wasn't learning to grind harder. It was realizing that living well is what fuels working well. I was starving myself of life and wondering why I was weak."

*
**

As Jacob discovered, postponing life until "success" kills both life *and* success.

You might be delaying the very things that would make you more effective, creative, and resilient. This chapter will show you how to start living fully *now* while still building for tomorrow.

You may recall Graysen's and my trip to the Philippines. We had delayed our vacations to keep working on our business, yet the trip became a turning point not just in our lives but in the lives of people in Lapu-Lapu City. Three days in, I was crawling out of my skin from boredom. We needed to take action.

That restlessness is what led us to Mia's sari-sari shop—the village's Quick Mart that had been in sad shape for years. With our "vacation budget" repurposed into micro-philanthropy, we helped reopen the store and set it up to flourish. Within weeks, its profits were feeding kids at the local church.

None of that would have been possible without Graysen and me taking that trip.

The In-Order-To Trap

In-order-to-ing is the biggest lie out there. *I'll be happy when I hit six figures. I'll relax when the business is stable. I'll call Mom when the gigs slow down.* Those are just pleas to postpone taking action. And it will bleed you dry.

I learned that the hard way back in 2017. FlashPants was booming with 200 shows a year, money flowing, crowds screaming. But I was miserable. I told myself: *I'll relax when we hit 300 shows. I'll take a break when we're settled. I'll be okay once we cross the next milestone.*

Meanwhile, I missed weddings, birthdays, and my own health. I was starving in the present, chasing crumbs of a future that never arrived.

Why Living Now Fuels Stacking Later

Conventional wisdom has it backward. Living now doesn't compete with stacking later, it powers it.

After that Philippines trip, we came back sharper, more creative, and more connected to *why* we were building in the first place. That so-called "wasted" time gave us:

- A micro-philanthropy project that became a blueprint for future giving
- Fresh concepts for scaling our businesses: ideas that surfaced only because we slowed down
- Recharged energy that fueled months of productivity
- Strategic clarity that made decision-making easier and faster

The lesson? Taking action isn't selfish. It's the prerequisite for success.

The Four Principles of Living Now While Stacking Later

Principle 1: Energy Is Your True Currency

Your most valuable resource isn't time. It's energy.

Work 16 hours at 30% capacity, and you get the equivalent of 4.8 hours of real productivity. Work 8 hours at 90% capacity, and you get 7.2.

Living now is about managing energy, not just clocking hours:

- Take breaks that actually restore you
- Do things that energize instead of drain you
- Recognize rest as productive, not lazy
- Invest in experiences that refill your creative tank

Principle 2: Present-Moment Awareness Improves Everything

When you're locked into the moment, everything upgrades:

- Business decisions get sharper
- Creative solutions show up naturally
- Relationships deepen and strengthen

- Learning accelerates because you're engaged

I saw this firsthand teaching trading. The days I rushed through lessons, thinking about what was next, were always my worst. When I was fully present with students, not only did they learn more. I learned more about teaching.

Principle 3: Joy Is a Skill That Stacks

Joy isn't a perk you get after success, it's a competitive edge that creates success.

People who enjoy the process:

- Stick with it longer when obstacles hit

- Find more creative solutions

- Attract better opportunities and partners

- Build systems that last instead of burning out

Joy isn't the reward for winning. Joy is how you win.

Principle 4: Your Best Work Comes From Abundance, Not Scarcity

You can't pour from an empty cup. If you're depleted, desperate, or exhausted, that energy bleeds into your work.

When you're fed, rested, connected, and engaged, the quality is night and day, more innovative, more confident, more persuasive.

That's why the Philippines trip didn't derail our businesses, it strengthened them. We came back operating from abundance, not fumes.

How Living Now Transfers to Everything

Business Development

When you're not desperate for every deal, you can choose the *right* ones. When your energy is full, you see opportunities others miss.

Examples:

- A consultant who takes sabbaticals returns with fresh perspective, and lands bigger clients than nonstop grinders.

- An entrepreneur who cultivates hobbies outside of business builds skills and networks that unexpectedly benefit the company.

Relationship Building

Exhaustion makes you a worse partner, friend, or colleague. Fullness makes you magnetic.

Examples:

- Making time for date nights or friend hangouts, even during busy seasons, creates bonds that hold strong when times get rough.

- Being fully present in conversations deepens trust and sparks opportunities you couldn't script.

Health and Longevity

Living today means treating your body like an investment in long-term performance, not as a drag on short-term productivity.

Examples:

- Recreational exercise done consistently beats occasional grueling workouts.

- Cooking food you enjoy instead of relying on fast food boosts energy now *and* builds long-term resilience.

Skill Development

Fullness accelerates learning. Exhaustion blocks it.

Examples:

- Tackling fun projects teaches you faster and sticks longer than grinding through uninspired coursework.

- Taking time off to explore "unrelated" interests often leads to surprising skill combinations you can't get from a straight line.

The False Choice

Most people think they must pick between *living today* and *building for tomorrow.* That's a false dilemma.

The real choice is:

- **Depletion path:** unsustainable, low quality, joyless

- **Fullness path:** high quality, sustainable, energizing

When you live now while stacking later, you gain:

- More energy for the things that matter

- Sharper judgment about what's worth doing

- Greater resilience in hard seasons

- Higher creativity and problem-solving ability

- Stronger relationships that fuel your goals

- A life filled with more meaning and joy

Reinvention Skill Spotlight: Present-Moment Productivity

Living now while stacking later isn't about balance, it's about integration. Here's how to stack this skill:

- **Energy Auditing:** Track what drains you vs. what fuels you, and schedule accordingly.

- **Present-Moment Practices:** Train yourself to fully engage with whatever you're doing right now.

- **Joy Integration:** Make necessary work enjoyable instead of just tolerable.

- **Strategic Rest:** Use rest and recreation as *investments* in future performance, not as escapes from work.

- **Fullness Creation:** Regularly do things that fill your tank so you can pour from overflow.

Chapter 22 Activity: Design Your Live Now, Stack Later System

Time to combine present-moment living with strategic building.

Step 1: *In-Order-To* Audit

Spot where you're postponing life:

- What do you tell yourself you'll do *"when"* you accomplish X?

- What activities are you holding off until some milestone?

- Where are you stuck in prep mode instead of life mode?

- What would you do this month if your income never increased?

Step 2: Energy Investment Analysis

Track your energy for a week. Separate what fuels you from what drains you.

Energizers:

- What makes you more alive and creative?
- What leaves you replenished instead of drained?
- When do you do your best work?

Drainers:

- What always leaves you flat?
- Where are you just going through the motions?
- What "shoulds" eat your energy without serving your goals?

Step 3: Opportunities for Integration

Find ways to live now while still building later.

Work Integration:

- How can you make necessary work more enjoyable?
- What changes if you approach goals with curiosity instead of obligation?
- Where could you be more present during routine tasks?

Life Integration:

- What life experiences would sharpen your work?
- How can you nurture relationships without seeing them as distractions?
- What hobbies or fun projects could double as valuable skills?

Step 4: Present-Moment Practices

Anchor yourself in today through deliberate routines.

Morning Practice:

- How will you start the day grounded in the present?
- What reminds you today matters, not just the future?

Work Practice:

- How will you stay engaged in the process, not just chase the result?

- What makes necessary tasks feel more meaningful?

Evening Practice:

- How will you acknowledge what you accomplished today?

- What helps you switch from work mode back to life mode?

Wrapping It Up

Quit waiting for permission to live. Quit postponing joy until you've "earned" it. Quit treating today as just a stepping stone. Your life is happening right now. Your best work comes from fullness, not depletion. Your sharpest ideas surface when you're energized, not burned out.

Live now, stack later isn't about choosing between short-term joy and long-term achievement. It's about realizing they fuel each other.

So, take the trip. Call your parents. Clean your apartment. Cook a real meal. Show up for the people who matter. Not because you have extra time. But because these moments will make you stronger at everything you're building.

The future doesn't belong to those who sacrifice life to "arrive." It belongs to those present enough in each moment to build a future worth living.

CONCLUSION
STACK ON

Y ou made it.

Twenty-two chapters. Thousands of words. Dozens of stories, frameworks, and exercises designed to help you turn any crisis into fuel for what comes next.

But here's the truth about endings: they're just beginnings in disguise.

This book is not the finish line. It's the map. And the journey doesn't end because the person who can stack skills, endure crucibles, and reinvent themselves isn't someone you become once. It's someone you keep becoming every time life demands more than you currently are.

What You Now Know

If you've made it this far, you've grasped something most people never do:

- **Crises are not the enemy of growth. They're the catalysts.** Every problem either destroys you or forges you stronger. The difference? Whether you know how to extract value from adversity.

- **Skills aren't just job qualifications. They're life amplifiers.** When you stack skills strategically—performance with analysis, imagination with structure, compassion with leadership—you don't just become more employable. You become more *alive.*

- **Reinvention is not abandoning your past. It's integrating it.** The healer's empathy, the entertainer's presence, the entrepreneur's systems, the teacher's clarity—they don't vanish. They stack. They evolve. They merge into the person you're becoming next.

The Stacking Never Stops

After four decades of shifting from real estate to music, performing to teaching, entrepreneurship to writing (and now inventing), I've learned one thing: the stack never ends.

Just when you think you've perfected the mix, life throws a new crucible. It forces you to recombine, to expand, to evolve into something beyond what you imagined.

That's not a flaw in the process. That's the design.

The goal isn't to "arrive" at some perfect version of yourself and coast. The goal is to become the type of person who thrives on reinvention.

The type of person who feels *excited, not terrified* when life demands another level-up, who sees every crisis not as punishment, but as raw material for the next transformation.

Stack your way forward. Again. And again. And again. Because reinvention isn't a one-time act. It's your way of life.

Your Next Crucible Is Coming

I'm not saying this to scare you. I'm saying it to prepare you.

Industries will shift. Relationships will change. Health challenges will surface. Economies will fluctuate. Technology will disrupt what you think you've mastered.

The question isn't *if* you'll face another crucible. The question is whether you'll be ready to use it as fuel for your next evolution.

And unlike most people, you now have an edge:

- A framework for turning chaos into capability
- A system for extracting skills from every experience
- A method for stacking those skills into something exponentially more powerful

The Three Ways Forward

Path 1: Go Back to Sleep

Do what you've done with every other book—get hyped for a week, try a couple exercises, then slip back into old patterns. Wait for the next crisis to force change instead of owning it. Keep believing reinvention is something that happens *to* you.

It's safe. It's familiar. It's also a waste of everything you just learned.

Path 2: Optimize Your Current Stack

Apply the frameworks here to make your current life better.

- Use the skill preservation system to protect what you've built.
- Use the health-wealth stack to sustain long-term success.
- Use the power of "no" to guard your energy.

This path works. It will improve your life. But it's not transformation. It's optimization.

Path 3: Stack Your Way to Reinvention

Choose deliberate evolution.

- Decide which skills you need to build the life you want.
- Shape the crucibles that will forge those skills.
- Weave everything you learn into a master stack that's yours alone.

This path is harder. Less certain. More demanding. But it's the only one that delivers exponential growth.

Your First Next Step

If you choose Path 3—and I hope you do—here's your assignment:

Go back to Chapter 1 and retake the Triage Test, not because your life hasn't changed (I'm sure it has), but because you have.

A few weeks ago, a crisis was just that. Today, it may look like an opportunity. When you began this book, you may have been facing what felt like a dead end. With the tools and tactics you've earned here, it may now look like a chance to pivot into a new career, a new outlook, a new and improved version of yourself.

You are no longer the same person who cracked open this book. You now have new frameworks, new lenses, and new possibilities.

Look at your current situation with fresh eyes and ask yourself:

What if this isn't happening *to* me, but *for* me?
What skills is this situation asking me to cultivate?
How can I stack my way through this circumstance instead of just surviving it?

Better yet, these are the exact types of questions Living Book Technology™ is being built to help you explore.

As the platform becomes available, it is designed to allow you to interact with the spirit of this book—asking questions, consulting the lessons, working through the frameworks, and applying the concepts directly to your life. The system is intended to guide you through each lesson and activity step by step, helping you take a clear inventory of where you are, what you already know, and what to build next.

The lessons won't stay locked away in these pages. Over time, you'll be able to apply the ideas and frameworks in a way that is tailored to your situation, your interests, and your schedule. The result is a comprehensive reinvention system and actionable plan designed to reveal who you truly are and move you toward where you're destined to go.

Living Book Technology™ is designed to do the heavy lifting—synthesizing your skills, experiences, and real-world scenarios into a clear, personalized blueprint of where you are now and where you're going.

The Ripple Effect

Here's what I've learned after decades of living this process:

When you start stacking strategically, it doesn't just transform your life. It transforms the lives around you.

Your family sees a new model for handling adversity. Your friends watch someone refuse to stagnate. Your coworkers experience what it's like to work alongside someone who treats problems as training grounds.

You become proof that reinvention is possible. And in a world where most people feel trapped, that's a radical act of service.

The Long Game

Skill stacking isn't a quick fix. It's a lifelong practice.

- The skills you build in your 20s set the foundation for your 40s.

- The trials you overcome in your 40s prepare you for success in your 60s.

- The wisdom you gain in your 60s becomes the legacy you leave behind.

Every skill stacks. Every experience compounds. Every reinvention equips you for the next.

That's how you create a life that bends under pressure without breaking. That's how you build resilience that outlasts markets, industries, and setbacks. That's how you become antifragile.

Your Story Continues

This book ends here. But your journey doesn't.

You now have the frameworks. The stories. The exercises.

The only thing missing is you.

Do you have the courage to treat your current challenge as a laboratory for new skills? To integrate what you've learned into your own system? To stack your way toward a life that gets more interesting—not less—as time goes on?

Your crucible is waiting. Your skills are ready. The only question left is: What are you going to build?

The end is the beginning.

Start stacking.

GLOSSARY OF UNIQUE TERMS & CONCEPTS

Core Stacking Concepts

- **Skill Stacking**: The strategic combination of multiple abilities that create exponential value rather than merely additive results. Not just having diverse skills, but deliberately integrating them so each amplifies the others.

- **The Master Stack**: The highest level of skill integration where all your abilities function as a unified system, producing outcomes uniquely yours that no one else can replicate.

- **Skill Half-Life**: The rate at which unused skills decay. Without maintenance or integration, abilities deteriorate faster than most people realize, requiring strategic preservation.

- **Skill Preservation System**: The strategic framework for maintaining and integrating abilities over time so they don't decay. Includes active practice, teaching others, cross-application, and deliberate integration into new contexts. Prevents skill half-life from eroding hard-won capabilities.

- **Premium Skills**: High-leverage capabilities created by combining 3+ foundational or mid-tier skills. These rare combinations produce disproportionate results (e.g., leadership in entertainment = performance + systems + sales + team management).

- **Skill Agility**: The ability to rapidly adapt existing skills to new contexts or combine them in novel ways when circumstances shift. Speed and flexibility in skill application and transfer.

Crisis & Reinvention Terms

- **The Crucible**: A period of intense pressure or adversity designed to transform rather than destroy. Context that burns away the false and forges what's real.

- **The Myth of Arrival**: The false belief that struggle ends at some imaginary finish line. Reality: there is no arrival, only evolution and new challenges at higher levels.

- **The Single Skill Trap**: Over-reliance on one ability or career path that leaves you vulnerable when industries, economies, or circumstances shift.

- **911 Emergency / Drive to ER / Urgent Care / Wellness Check**: Four-level crisis triage system for accurately diagnosing life situations and matching appropriate responses (Chapter 1 framework).

- **The Blank Page Moments**: When everything false has burned away and you're left with nothing—which paradoxically becomes the foundation for authentic reinvention.

- **Crisis as Catalyst**: Reframing adversity not as punishment but as accelerated training that forges skills impossible to develop in comfort.

Identity & Operating Systems

- **Emotional Flexibility**: The ability to feel disappointment without being crushed by it, to take rejection without making it personal, and to keep moving even when progress is invisible. A critical meta-skill developed through repeated exposure to adversity.

- **The Rich Bro/Sis**: A partner or mentor rich in vision, foresight, and strategic thinking (not necessarily money) who thinks 5-10 years ahead and helps you level up your operating system.

- **Strategic Vulnerability**: Deliberately choosing to reveal uncertainty, limitations, or learning-in-progress in order to build trust, invite collaboration, and accelerate growth.

- **Complex Simplification:** Turning abstract and difficult ideas into clear, simple, and concrete ones, using analogies, examples, rules of thumb, and straightforward language.

- **Identity Transfer**: Absorbing capabilities and perspectives from partners/ mentors until they become integrated into your own identity and decision-making.

- **MDD (Man Deficit Disorder)**: Humorous term for gaps in practical, manual skills that create insecurity. Represents any area where you feel incomplete or underprepared.

- **The Healer's Fork**: Decision point where you choose between different life paths, recognizing that "not chosen" doesn't mean "wasted"—skills from the unchosen path still transfer.

- **The Provider Instinct**: Deep-rooted drive to contribute and bring value, often formed in early childhood experiences of wanting to help family.

- **In-Order-To-ing**: The mental pattern of justifying present actions by their future payoff ("I'm doing X in order to get Y"). While useful for goal-setting, over-reliance on this mindset can prevent presence and appreciation of current experience. The antidote is learning to find value in the action itself, not just its instrumental outcome.

Performance & Presence Terms

- **Stage Presence (as transferable skill)**: Ability to command attention and make everyone feel directly addressed. Transfers from entertainment to business, teaching, leadership, sales.

- **Micro-*noes***: tiny, deliberate "no" decisions that eliminate distractions, options, or commitments before they accumulate.

- **Strategic Generalist:** someone who keeps access to a wide range of abilities while sharpening concentrated expertise.

- **The Entertainer's Edge**: Five-skill combination: stage presence, timing, energy management, audience reading, and network building that creates magnetic influence in any domain.

- **Pattern Interrupts**: Strategic moments of unexpected content or energy shifts (Shake Weight competitions, Gangnam Style) designed to recapture wandering attention.

- **Reading the Room**: Real-time pattern recognition applied to human behavior and group energy. Sensing engagement, resistance, confusion, or readiness in seconds.

- **Energy Management (as leadership skill)**: Ability to raise or lower the emotional temperature of a space deliberately. Being the thermostat, not the thermometer.

Business & Systems Concepts

- **The Entrepreneur's Formula**: Five meta-skills: problem identification, solution design, risk management, team building, and systems creation. What separates business builders from service providers.

- **Micro-Philanthropy (expanded)**: Not just small giving—surgical application of resources at maximum leverage points where few others are looking.

- **Systems Creation**: Building processes that run without your constant presence. Difference between having a job and having a business.

- **The Lead Generation Business**: Recognition that most businesses aren't really about their apparent product—they're about systematically attracting qualified prospects.

- **Cloneable Systems**: Processes documented clearly enough that anyone can execute them with consistent quality, enabling true scale.

- **Intuition Stacking**: The practice of following subtle internal nudges without requiring logical justification upfront. Each time you honor intuition and discover it led somewhere valuable, you build trust in the signal. Over time, this creates a compounding advantage. Your intuition gets sharper because you actually use it, and opportunities appear that pure logic would have missed.

Relationship & Connection Terms

- **The Connector's Code:** Five skills that build real relationships: forming lasting bonds, trust creation, community development, vulnerability, and leadership through service.

- **Familiar Souls**: Relationships that don't require maintenance contracts—you can go months without contact and reconnect instantly without guilt or obligation.

- **Scorekeepers**: People who measure friendship in unpaid invoices, treating relationships as transactional debts rather than genuine connection.

- **Brotherhood/Sisterhood (through shared struggle)**: Bonds accelerated through joint adversity rather than casual socializing. Forged in crucibles, not cocktail parties.